D1596512

Praise For Thrive

"A must read if you want to go from surviving to thriving! - If you are going through or recovering from heartbreak, then Julie Bishop is the heartfelt friend, the thoughtful teacher and inspiring role model that we all want and need. In Thrive Anyway, Julie addresses the feelings and phases that you encounter when going through loss. She generously shares her stories, as well as insightful practices, exercises and "how-to" tips so you will emerge empowered and better than ever! A must read if you want to go from surviving to thriving!"

- Kelley Kosow, The Ford Institute
www.kelleykosow.com

"WOW, so proud of you and excited for you!"

-Michael Port, New York Time Best Selling
Author "Book Yourself Solid", MichaelPort.com

"Compassionate, real and full of actionable wisdom, 'Thrive Anyway' is a healing salve for anyone ready to bravely move forward after heartbreak."

- Jenny Fenig, Coach and Author of "*Get Gutsy*",
JennyFenig.com

"Thank you for getting this kind of work out there in this way."

- Clifford Edwards,
Author of *The Forgiveness Handbook*
www.theforgivenesshandbook.com

"An invaluable recovery guide for a broken heart! Thrive Anyway is the perfect book for anyone who has or is experiencing a painful loss, particularly divorce… A clear cut map through heartbreak … Innovative techniques and strategies for dealing with the harmful effects of stress… May this book find its way to all who are in need of it."

- Lynne Glazer, Divorce Mediator,
Best Choice Divorce

Julie knows whereof she speaks; not just because she has faced tribulations, but because she figured out how to transform them. She encourages us all to have a kick-ass life, giving the why as well as the how. Thrive Anyway is a thorough, well-researched, and lovingly crafted how-to for healing your heart."

- Mikka Baloy, Shamanic Teacher,
www.shamanmikki.com

I love this book…a kind-hearted, compassionate and ultimately practical book filled with wisdom born out of experience, which is the best kind of wisdom. It leads us back to ourselves, which is the best place to be when we want to start over.

- MaryJane Aboud, owner of
This Is Your Life Coaching

"Thrive Anyway, provides easily accessible and effective ways to move through the huge transitions and heartbreak of life's major challenges in a way that builds confidence and allows people to access their own deeper resources. Instead of languishing in a pool or resentments and disappointment, her readers find ways to "thrive anyway", to transform and blossom into who they are beyond their wildest dreams. A must read for anyone moving through the traumas of divorce."

- Mary Campbell, Spiritual/Sexual Educator and Counselor, Certified Exceptional Marriage Mentor, and Inter-Spiritual Minister www.diviningbeauty.com

"Compliments to the way this book outlines the nine stages of grief after the end of a relationship and the superbly practical activities suggested within each phase to support healing. As I read I could clearly identify with each…and the paralyzing effects this can have on anyone. As the author writes "heartbreak is non-discriminatory". This book touched on so many emotions and especially the ones that people, myself included, have found to be difficult to understand let alone talk about… This is an extraordinary value - clean, clear & easy to understand… "

- Cameron Comstock, Artist and Author of,
"The Adventures of Menlow Parker"

Thrive

ANYWAY

Discover How To Heal Your Broken Heart from Divorce or a Bad
Breakup: Recover from the 9 Stages of Grief, Manage
Stress & Anxiety, and Create Healthy Relationships
for a Happier Healthier YOU!

JULIE ANNA BISHOP

Big Ripple Publishing, USA

Big Ripple Publishing

207 N. Plain Road
Great Barrington, MA 01230

Julie Anna Bishop, julieannabishop.com

Barnum Media Group
www.BarnumMedia.com

Warning – Disclaimers

The purpose of this book is to educate, inspire and entertain. The author and/or publisher do not guarantee that anyone following these techniques, suggestions, tips, ideas, or strategies will become successful. The author and/or publisher shall have neither liability nor responsibility to anyone with respect to any loss or damage caused, or alleged to be caused, directly or indirectly by the information contained in this book.

The author of this book does not dispense medical advice, diagnosis, nor prescribe the use of any technique as the form of treatment for physical, mental, medical or emotional problems without the advice of a physician, either directly or indirectly. The intent of the author is only to offer information of a general nature to help you on your quest for emotional and spiritual well-being. The author and publisher assume no responsibility for your actions.

Dedication

Barbara Baker and Glenn Bishop

Thank you for raising, loving and
believing in me even when I
tested the limits of your parenthood.
Thank you for my first experience of divorce.
You dwell in my heart daily, and I look forward to
joining you someday in the hereafter.

To all of my teachers (past & future)
in the realm of intimate relationships:

You know who you are. I'm deeply grateful. I wish you all a thriving, fulfilling
and meaningful life. Xoxo

Contents

.

Acknowlegements

To my sisters and brothers as well as their spouses:

You always jump in to help others;
You support me always.
Each of you is absolutely amazing.
Thank you for being you. xoxo

To my children:

You are by far the most
incredible inspirations
and loves of my life;
excellent teachers, friends
and individuals.
You're the best! Xoxo

To my Safeplan advocate - Karen:

You held me on many levels in court and throughout the court restraint process:
I am ever grateful. Xoxo

I Am Free

I stand on the precipice of thriving,
Perched on the edge of the cliff,
Fingers outstretched to the light,
The shadows seep in from behind,
Single wrist bound,
The past beckons backwards,
The choice is mine,
Two very different worlds let go,
Surrendered to the moment,
Open my heart,
Trust,
Flourish,
Fly,
Spread my wings and love,
I refuse to fall,
I won't get lost again,
I will not be abandoned,
I will fly,
I will be,
I will thrive,
The light will catch me,
I am free.

~Ericka Wilcox, personal text, 2015

In order to
kick ass
you must first
lift up your foot.

-Jen Sincero, *You Are a Baddass:
How To Stop Doubting Your Greatness
And Start Living An Awesome Life*

CHAPTER 1

Introduction Letter

(How To Get The Most Out Of This Book)

To You -

Congratulations on your first courageous step toward taking care of your needs, getting on with your life, and healing your heart! Just for making this step, I want to give you kick-ass bonus gifts that will bring more joy, relaxation and self-love (self-value) to your healing process. You can take a moment to download your free bonus of 50 self-care action steps: http://www.thriveanywaybook.com/bonuses.

Whatever your situation may be that broke your heart- I want first to tell you that you are not alone. Relationships end every few seconds, all across the world. Which means there are thousands of relationship breakdowns every day; any relationship between two individuals can come to an end. Broken relationships include those between relatives, friends, colleagues, lovers or business partners. No matter where you live, what race you are or what language you speak, the disempowering effects of a broken relationship do not discriminate. No one is impervious to its reach. It would seem that just about everyone in this world has experienced an end of a relationship at one time or another and the broken heart that goes with it.

I realize that knowing you are not alone while comforting, is not enough to ease your pain. This book was created with the intention to help support you in taking conscious action while caring for yourself. During the next few weeks and month, it is critical that you care for yourself as you heal your heart to live your best life and create even healthier relationships moving forward.

Like you, I have experienced the immense stress, pain, and angst that occurs at the end of a significant relationship numerous times throughout my life. One of the most challenging of these happened at the end of my twenty-year marriage. Compounding the stress was being unemployed, becoming a single mother of two and experiencing the dark side of my former spouse's struggle with the end of our marriage. To be completely truthful, it was extremely difficult at first. I shut down almost completely, I couldn't eat, sleep, or work. I barely could care for myself, my children and the pets. I was also fearful that there may be retaliations that would bring additional harm to me or my kids.

In fact, I lived in a constant state of stress, fear and deep sadness for the first few months after he was removed from our home. I found myself on public assistance, selling everything I had of value just to pay minimal bills and put food on the table. As hard as it was, those experiences ultimately taught me about my inner strength. Within me lay resilience, capability of healthy boundaries, courage, and compassion.

Almost as challenging were events that took place twenty-five years ago in my late teens. Between my junior and senior year of high school, my mother passed away. I believed her aggressive cancer was due partially to her inability to handle the aftermath of stress and emotions that accompanied the end of her twenty-nine-year marriage. My beliefs about her death put a large wedge in my relationship with my father, who had separated from my mother three years prior.

Worsening the ability to heal from her death was the loss of three lovers; one who broke off our relationship the day of my mother's funeral and two years later died in a motorcycle accident. The other young man I had dated off and on since I was fourteen stood by me through her death. I reluctantly let go of him during my freshmen year of college because the distance was too great for a charming young man that broke my heart in three months. I first *spiraled into depression and despair. Slowly I began to delve into different methods to ease the pain - therapy, prayer, journaling, volunteering, sports, hobbies, schoolwork, isolation, etc. Some of these methods were useful, others - not so productive.*

Weeding through what helped and what didn't, I was on a mission to be happy and healthy. Step by step, I unknowingly developed or tapped into one of my greatest gifts, the ability to transform my tragedies and painful experiences into opportunities to grow and blossom. My success had a great deal to do making a conscious decision to thrive and a cultivating a positive perspective. You may not think right now that you have this within you, but we all do. Each one of us can learn to turn our difficulties into an opportunity to evolve and find our freedom.

When it came to facing the completion of my marriage that I struggled to hold onto for so long, it was no different. Although I was a wreck in those first few months; acknowledging emotional abuse I lived in denial about; watching my former partner come apart at the seams and requiring a restraining order; living with overwhelming stress - I finally decided that self-pity and fear weren't getting me where I desired to go. In fact, this victim dynamic had paralyzed me at a time that action would have been more beneficial. I realized a different approach was required.

I recalled my earlier struggles and how I managed them. Instead of beating myself up for things I felt I should have done, which would have been self-defeating and unhelpful, I acknowledged myself for the difficulty of this transition. I made a promise to myself that I was going to get myself and my children through this experience. I reached out to others and supported myself to take conscious, empowering action.

Over the next six months, I began to take responsibility for my part in the breakdown of the relationship. Creating support around my damaged self-esteem, instilling firm boundaries, and taking control of my emotions that had been running rampant, I found outlets that nurtured my soul. Remembering that I was in control of how I reacted, what I was feeling and the choices I was making allowed me to begin to heal and find my footing. Being gentle and patient with myself was crucial.

I remember realizing that no one was coming to save me. The only way to heal was to meet my fears, grief and pain head on and move through them for myself. Being a survivor of trauma several times over, I knew I could do it again using tools I had learned along the way. Many of which I had gathered in the past seven years of studying to become an Integrative Coach at The Ford Institute for Transformational Training. Taking difficulties and turning them into sources of empowerment is the answer. These are the tools shared with you throughout this book.

As a certified bodyworker and an Integrative Courage Coach™, my clients and I partner in their healing process with incredible results. I put my advice and guidance into action for myself. Before I knew it, my family and friends began to remark on how well I was doing and how great I looked. I shared the techniques I was using in service of other men and women who found themselves in the same or similar positions. When others found these methods and techniques extremely helpful, getting consistently positive results, I realized many people could benefit. I wrote this book from that place of compassion. May this book and your particular crisis become catalysts for you to take back your power and your life. May your stress be reduced and may your broken heart be a springboard for better health and a more fulfilling life. You deserve it.

The beauty of your situation is that you can take control of yourself, your actions, your words and your emotions instead of allowing them to control you. How you cope with your loss is truly up to you. In fact, it is what you decide to do with it and how you handle it that determines how quickly you heal. Who doesn't want to streamline the process and avoid getting stuck in their sorrow? Just by picking up this book assures you that you are ready to move through this experience and heal your heart.

While our instincts may pull us to avoid, ignore or otherwise seek the easiest way in dealing with our pain head on, the healthiest way is to embrace the kick-ass courageous warrior that dwells within you. Tapping into that inner courage and healing energy enables you to face your fears one at a time and go through the grieving process with grace, strength and ease. I won't promise you it will be easy, but I know for sure it will be worth it.

Not all of the information or exercises in this book will resonate with you. I suggest that you read through it once without doing the exercises— take notice and highlight the ones that speak to you. Circle back to the ones that sparked your interest once you've digested the contents and begin there. In the resource section, there are suggested books, links to various other works and audio recordings to further assist you in your healing process. With a little bit of trust, willingness and action, you will soon be coping, healing and yes, even thriving. It may not seem like it to you, but I honestly believe if my friends, clients and I can heal using these methods, so can you.

By the end of this book, it is my hope that you will be able to embrace a liberating perspective in regards to the end of your relationship. This ending is your new beginning; an opportunity to learn something valuable about yourself, release beliefs that no longer serve you and fuel your personal growth. You have within you, the ability to redefine who you are, who shares your life and how you want to live it.

You don't have to create this new beginning alone either. Now is the time in your life to also begin to connect and reach out to others who may be facing the very same grief and changes you are currently experiencing. By the end of *this book, you will be ready to look within your circle of friends and within the greater community for ways to connect to new people that are going to be more than happy to cheer you on, offer an ear or shoulder to lean on and have your back.*

In addition to this book, I have included extra bonuses; guided meditations, mantras, nutritional guidelines, and fifty proven action steps to positively engage in to lift your spirits. You can use both to discover the kick ass courageous warrior within you that is ready to be activated. You can tap into a deeper strength, wisdom, and power to heal your broken heart. Sending you much joy, love, and intention for creating your internal happiness and complete well-being. Don't forget to download your free gifts and to believe in yourself, because I certainly do-
With love,

P.S. In the spirit of one of my mentors and esteemed colleagues, Michael Port - New York Best Selling Author of Book Yourself Solid as well as Author and founder of The Think Big Revolution, I am borrowing his disclaimer when it comes to errors. "May my spelling and grammar errors be my gift to you."

You Can and You Will Thrive if
That is Your Deepest Desire!

Throughout this book there are numerous exercises,
exploratory questions, and suggestions for reflection
as well as a plan of action at the end of each chapter.
To further support you in making the most of your
healing experience, we have created an exclusive
Thrive Anyway "Clarity Journal.". With this tool, you
can use your heartache as a kick-ass catalyst for
achieving your extraordinary life. Your first action step
will be to download your journal so you can get
started on the path to more certainty, joy and
confidence.

If you haven't already downloaded your Thrive
Anyway Clarity Journal Go Now To:
www.thriveanywaybook.com

Begin Creating Your Happier Healthier You!

I'm not going
to promise you it
will be easy, but
I know for sure
it will be worth it.

- Julie Bishop,
*"Thrive Anyway:You Can
Heal Your Broken Heart"*

CHAPTER 2

Why Divorce and Break Ups Are So Stressful

F irst and foremost, heartbreak is extremely stressful because there is a deeply painful emotional loss. The end of a relationship is one of the most stressful things that can happen to you, next to losing someone to death. If it isn't your first time, the pain of old wounds are re-opened, and your experience compounded. Divorce is one of the worst of all heartbreak. If you are like me, you entered your marriage intending it be a forever bond and have done everything you can to make it work before making the difficult decision to divorce. Marriage represents a coming together of soulmates, one where you love, honor, and cherish your partner for a lifetime.

Marriage is the embodiment of two people become one, it's not just it is not just a physical bond, it's one of an emotional and spiritual one as well. The shattering of this bond makes divorce the most entangled and difficult of all breakups. There is a ceremony, a promise to one another, For woman next to being a mother, it's the biggest commitment you make in your lifetime. Divorce breaks that promise, creating a ripple effect through your families, loved ones and community, that is felt through your entire being.

It's not just about having the person no longer there; it is also about losing someone that has been your close friend. You had a great deal invested in this relationship, and now all the dreams and commitments you've shared are gone. And on some level, it may leave you wondering if you somehow weren't good enough, that you may never find someone who loves you for you, or that there is something wrong with you. It can be a lonely and dis-empowering place to be. For many, being alone can bring up a lot of fear and be downright terrifying. There are hurt feelings, anger and unspoken communications that weigh on your mind and your heart.

The end of a relationship also launches you into uncharted territory disrupting your whole life. Your dynamics and other relationships are affected. Routines, responsibilities, living arrangements, children, the circle of friends, family, ex-partner's family, possibly even your identity is impacted, altered or severed. Literally, your world is turned upside down and sideways. Your breakup can

trigger many unsettling feelings of grief, loss, shame, and despair– building up a great deal of stress and anxiety.

There is many types of divorce advice you can get before, during or after your divorce while navigating this uncharted territory. The legal divorce advice will guide you through the divorce laws of your state; sorting the difficulties of dividing assets, determining the terms of custody, and ensuring you are informed of your rights. Then there is family and friend divorce advice,some helpful, some not so helpful. Often you will wear each other out in the process which leads you to seek profession divorce counseling and therapeutic divorce advice. What divorce and separation family law do not provide is the help you need emotionally, mentally and physically during, and after you have gone through the legal battle. At times, the aftermath of the divorce is the hardest part of your journey. This book is your resource, journal, and personal guide to healing.

On a physical level, you may experience loss of sleep, lack of appetite, and obsessive mental chatter you can't seem to stop. You may not feel motivated to go to work, get out of bed, or see anyone. In your mind, you are dwelling on who is to blame, what you could have done differently or beating yourself up for your perceived mistakes. Internally and externally, these experiences leave you physically and mentally vulnerable. It's no wonder your stress level is through the roof and in turn, your immune system suffers.

If you have been in an abusive or controlling relationship, you may even be scared of the other person's reaction to the breakup. While it may not mean that he or she was a "bad" person, it means the relationship was toxic to you and not healthy for your ex either. Part of you may know that and still have strong feelings for this person, making it hard to have a clean break. Seek the assistance of a professional in supporting you through the end of an emotionally or physically abusive relationship can be very helpful.

According to Lundy Bancroft, a relationship abuse expert, there are ten profiles of an abuser or combination thereof. Many abusers are so subtle you may not realize you have been a victim of their manipulation. Sometimes, you sense something is off, and may assume it is you. Often, because you love them, you suffer from traumatic bonding. The resource section at the end lists helpful books, including Lundy Bancroft's, that can help you determine if your ex-partner was abusive because there are specific things you will face and need to heal from that are different than a regular breakup.

If someone is stalking you, your boundaries are being crossed, or your requests ignored, that is abusive behavior. If you are receiving threats such as "If I can't have you, no one can" or "You are messing with the wrong person", reach out for support from the National Domestic Violence Hotline at 800-799-SAFE. You can call and remain anonymous if needed. They also have a website: http://www.thehotline.org/get-help/safety-planning/ with various kinds of information on safety planning.

Regardless of the circumstances of the end of your relationship, you will experience some level of stress. Everybody is looking for a magic wand, a fast way to heal or get over the heartbreak. No one can give you an instant, painless or stress-free way to get through this major bump in your road. What I can tell you is your breakup does not have to be traumatic or stay traumatic. You can take the initial sting out of your crisis with the proper knowledge and understanding of the entire process. It does not need to take one or even two years of emotional and physical stress to work through recovering from your broken relationship. To find the quickest way to a new, happy, and less stressful life it is helpful to have a clear understanding of how stress works and the multiple emotional phases of the grieving process.

You Can and You Will Thrive if
That is Your Deepest Desire!

Remember that this is a marathon, not a sprint so it is going to take some effort on your part. Every race starts with one small step. Be kind, gentle and patient with yourself as you begin the necessary steps to find peace and clarity for yourself. Now that you have an introduction to why breakups are so stressful it is time for some reflection in your journal. If you haven't downloaded your Thrive Anyway Clarity Journal yet, please take a moment to do so now. Your second action step will be to make some lists. Think of all the things that you are worried about, have fear around, and are stressing over. Put them down in your journal and answer the questions provided.

If you haven't already downloaded your Thrive Anyway Clarity Journal Go Now To:
www.thriveanywaybook.com

Creating Your Happier Healthier You!

All stress comes from resisting what is.

- Oprah Winfrey,
American Queen of Media

CHAPTER 3

The Truth About Stress and Anxiety

Your stress develops out the anguish of your loss and learning to manage it as well as your emotional grief is key to healing. Dealing with your stress initially begins to alleviate your pain. Unfortunately, we are often poorly prepared to deal with the effects of stress–most of us were not taught to cope or manage it in school, from our family or even society at large. Before discussing the helpful tools and techniques for handling stress, I'd like to highlight some of the information and research that supports why managing your stress is so crucial for your optimal well-being.

All types of stress affect your body. Inherently, perceived stressors trigger anxiety and other feelings that cause exhaustion, unexplained physical symptoms, and impaired immune systems. Consistent stressors leave you defenseless against everything from the common cold to the creation of the perfect internal environment for cancerous growth. Stress, while naturally occurring to some degree, when left unchecked is more dangerous than you may care to believe.

According to the American Psychological Association's Stress in America™ Survey, more than 9 in 10 (94 percent) of "adults believe that stress can contribute to the development of major illnesses, such as heart disease, depression and obesity, and that some types of stress can trigger heart attacks, arrhythmias, and even sudden death, particularly in people who already have cardiovascular disease (92 percent)."[1] While the majority of adults (in this study) understand stress has a powerful impact on health, a sizeable minority still think stress has only a slight or no impact on their physical health (31 percent) and mental health (36 percent).[2]

So, given that information, you've probably heard that stress can raise your blood pressure or increase the likelihood of a stroke, but

---

[1] American Psychological Association's Stress in America™ Survey, retrieved from http://www.apa.org/news/press/releases/stress/2014/stress-report.pdf and http://www.apa.org/news/press/releases/2015/02/money-stress.aspx February 4, 2015

[2] American Psychological Association's Stress in America™ Survey, retrieved from http://www.apa.org/news/press/releases/stress/2014/stress-report.pdf

did you know that according to the American Psychological Association's research, chronic stress interferes with the normal function of your body's immune system? Doctors agree that during chronic stress, the survival role of the digestive and immune systems slow down, take the back burner or in some cases, shut down.[3] According to Dr. Herbert Benson, MD (father of modern mind-body medicine and author of 11 books / 175 research papers), your immune system is impaired by stress caused at the end of a relationship. He discovered that the chances of coming down with a major illness the first year after divorce (or a major breakup) were 12 times as great as normal.[4] Preventing the breakdown that provides an internal environment prone to disease are why it is so important to start your healing process by reducing your stress levels.

In the opening, I mentioned some of the more common stress factors that come with the end of a relationship: fear of the unknown, financial strains, increased responsibility for children, inability to sleep, eating improperly to name just a few. But often you also lose the friends, family, colleagues, and support structures you had if they decide to back the person that is no longer your partner. Your sense of self-worth, self-esteem, and identity also

---

[3] American Psychological Association's Stress in America™ Survey, retrieved from http://www.apa.org/news/press/releases/stress/2014/stress-report.pdf

[4] Benson, Herbert (2010), Relaxation Revolution, New York, Scribner, Division of Simon & Schuster Inc.

take a blow. All the rejection triggers negative meaning making and beliefs about yourself that are disempowering. Identifying your physical, mental and social stressors is vital to creating your approach to well-being.

Statistics is quite helpful in obtaining a birds-eye view and those related to anxiety, stress and relationships are certainly eye opening. According to the Center for Disease Control, one in every eight Americans age 18 to 64 suffers from an anxiety disorder, and one in every ten American adults suffer from depression.[5] According to the Anxiety and Depression of America Association, it is estimated that 40 million American adults suffer from anxiety disorders.[6] Research conducted by the National Institute of Mental Health has shown "that anxiety disorders are the number one mental health issue among American women. Mental health is second in numbers only to alcohol and drug abuse by American men."[7]

Equally alarming is that every year there are over two million divorces in the United States, according to the national census,

---

[5] Center For Disease Control http://www.cdc.gov

[6] ADAA, Anxiety and Depression Association of American, retrieved from http://www.adaa.org/understanding-anxiety

[7] National Inst. of Mental Health, retrieved from http://www.nimh.nih.gov/index.shtml

which doesn't even include the breakup of non-marital relationships that we mentioned earlier.[8] Could there be any correlation between the breakdown in relationships and our national levels of anxiety? It seems highly likely that it is one of the several factors contributing to anxiety and stress. According to US statistics, between 40 and 50 percent of first marriages, 67 percent of second marriages and 73 percent of third marriages in the United States end in divorce.[9] Interestingly, feedback from those polled in The American Psychological Association's Stress in America™ Survey indicated that relationships were the source of 58 % of their stress.[10]

Our medical community has observed that anxiety and stress go hand in hand. In fact, one of the primary symptoms of stress is anxiety. While having some anxiety is perfectly normal, especially when going through a breakup, Doctor's tend to jump right to medicating the problem. Women suffer from anxiety and stress almost as twice as much as men.[11] Understanding how stress and anxiety are born as well as learning methods of transforming your relationship to them will help shift current statistics. We can each

---

[8] National census, retrieved from http://www.census.gov

[9] US statistics Center For Disease Control, retrieved from http://www.cdc.gov

[10] American Psychological Association's Stress in America™ Survey, retrieved from http://www.apa.org/news/press/releases/stress/2014/stress-report.pdf

[11] http://www.healthinsightstoday.com

do our part. Anxiety disorders are the most common mental illness in American, surpassing even depression in numbers. [12]

A doctor's typical response to is to medicate the symptom. Unfortunately, they often do not teach those of us suffering from anxiety tools and techniques to help manage and transform the source of stress causing the anxiety. According to Dr. Julie Holland, MD, author of Moody Bitches: The Truth about the Drugs You're Taking, the Sleep You're Missing, the Sex You're Not Having, and What's Really Driving You Crazy, anxiety disorders are over diagnosed and too many women are being told to medicate away their essential, authentic selves. [13] I am not saying either myself or Dr. Holland are advocating no drugs as there are cases in which individuals with severe anxiety disorders, borderline personality disorders, bi-polar disorders and similar need and benefit from medication.

Contrary to common belief, there are distinct differences between stress and anxiety. The pressures of life induce the stress we feel as we react to outside stimulus and processes through our inner belief system. Life stress producers include handling big workloads,

---

[12] ADDA, "Facts and Statistics," Anxiety and Depression Association of America, retrieved from

[13] Holland, Judy (2015), Moody Bitches: The Truth About the Drugs You're Taking, the Sleep You're Missing, the Sex You're Not Having, and What's Really Making You Crazy, New York, Penguin Press

making a big decision, or creating a big change. This pressure builds, as it is perceived in our mind and body, causing an adrenaline release that makes our hearts pound, blood pressure increase, muscles tense, and pupils dilate. If there is an extended stay of the hormone, it can cause depression, an increase in blood pressure as well as a myriad of other negative changes and effects. Your perception and response to an existing stress-causing factor determine the level of stress you experience. There is a variety of situations or thoughts that you choose to react to with frustration, anger, nervousness or anxiety. What is not stressful to one person can be stressful to another; it has to do with how the stimulus is received, internalized, and processed.

One of the negative effects of consistently reacting in a default stress response is anxiety. It is not good or bad in and of itself. It is a natural part of your mind and body that is giving you feedback about your life. We all experience certain levels of anxiety when there are major transitions or new events that we haven't dealt with before. Then there is extreme anxiety in which fear overcomes all emotions accompanied by worry and apprehension, often giving you the jitters, chest pains, dizziness, shortness of breath, and frequent panic attacks. At this level, it begins to affect your life and ability to function in the greater world. These symptoms are red flags and sign to get more support and help.

My fear-induced stress of finally telling my former partner that I felt our relationship was over is how my beliefs manifested in my first panic attack. In the middle of a pet store, while I was shopping with my children, I became dizzy and felt I needed to sit down. I quickly told the children I needed to eat fast and scooted them to a restaurant nearby where I gathered myself together while it passed. Fortunately, I had enough friends at the time that were prone to them, so I quickly figured out what was happening.

During my panic attack, I asked myself what belief, what thoughts, and what fears were going through my mind. I then asked myself the core question, one of Byron Katie's powerful questions from "The Work," "Is it true?!" (Spiritual leader, Byron Katie, is the bestselling author of Loving What Is, I Need Your Love: and A Thousand Names for Joy and founder of "The Work.") Then my question, "What can I do to support myself?" It was through this method, of going inward and listening to my internal wisdom, that I was able to relax and take control of my experience. To get through it, I stepped into it and did not resist, fight it or try to make it stop. Instead, I decided just to allow myself the process, and as I did this, it eased up entirely.

Anxiety is stress that continues after the initial stressor is gone. For me, the difficult conversation had already happened the night before, but the fears that fueled my anxiety grew steadily and created unease in my body long afterward. Anxiety is a feeling of apprehension or fear. My thought in the store that came before the attack was "how is this going to affect my children, will they hate me?" and moved to judgment about myself, "I am a horrible mother." Feelings of impending doom accompany this kind of fear. The source of the discomfort, self-judgement and pressure is not always so easily recognized, which can compound your distress.

Everyone experiences a bit of anxiety from time to time. When faced with stressful situations it builds intensity based on your disempowering beliefs; just before an exam, before speaking at a podium, before an interview or walking down the aisle. It is quite common to feel anxious in these situations. They are all unique opportunities to help us transform the beliefs that no longer serve us.

However, for many, anxiety can interfere with everyday life and thinking of them as opportunities are difficult to wrap one's mind around. If it is affecting your life, keeping you from everyday experiences, it is time to seek professional assistance. Excessive anxiety often occurs with other psychiatric conditions such as depression. Anxiety is abnormal or unhealthy when it is prolonged or severe. If anxiety happens in the absence of a stressful event, or it is interfering with everyday activities such as going to work, then professional help is needed. Just because it is considered abnormal, doesn't mean that there is something wrong with you, most often it just means that there is something beneath your conscious awareness that is fueling the anxiety and depression. If you can work with a professional to get to what is underneath - the belief, viewpoint, and fear that you are defaulting to - it will go a long way in easing the resulting anxiety or depression. You can even begin by asking yourself right now - What fear is fueling my anxiety? What can I do for myself? What do I need to know to shift this fear? And if you are unable to get the answer on your own, consider speaking with a professional to assist you.

Anxiety is often brought on by the ending of a relationship, particularly if the breakup is long, tumultuous, and drawn out. The presence of stress in your life and surrounding your loss can provide an internal environment that enables you to manifest your anxious thoughts. Many who suffer from anxiety disorders occupy their minds with excessive worry. Spinning over and over in your head regarding past incidents and problems with your ex, health, job, current events, and so forth. This anxiety is often self-induced as it's filtered through your internal belief system, your fears, and your judgments. Fears do not make anxiety less real. However, if you possess the ability to create unease from your beliefs, you also possess the capability to take control and release your fears. How powerful is that concept?!

It is important to point out that there are external factors that directly impact the development of anxiety that are not caused by your internal belief system. Certain drugs, both recreational and prescribed, can produce physical symptoms of anxiety due to either the side effects or withdrawal from the drug. Other contributors to anxiety are a poor diet, low levels of vitamin B12 or D, post-traumatic stress disorder (PTSD), hormonal imbalance, and in rare cases, an adrenal gland tumor. The positive aspect here is that with your awareness of these contributing factors, you can make informed decisions regarding your diet, your vitamin intake and responsible use of medication. If you are feeling exhausted even after plenty of sleep, reach out to your physician for a checkup and explain your symptoms.

I feel drugs, the quick solution many doctors and therapists opt for when addressing anxiety or depression isn't always the best path. Don't get me wrong, there are times and situations for prescriptions, and if one is suffering from an anxiety disorder, I am not telling them they shouldn't get relief through medication. For full disclosure, I took an anti-depressant for one month during the second time my former partner and I went through marriage counseling. I didn't want to leave any stone unturned in making this the impactful decision to leave so I took the advice of our therapist and tried it. The drug helped reduce the level of anxiety I experienced and gave me time, space, and calmness to proceed. We reconciled for another two years until I was able to identify some of the core dynamics that were unhealthy for us both that I wasn't willing to look at or deal with previously.

Several close people in my life have also benefited greatly from medication for their anxiety or depression and are still taking it. However, it seems for so many, as Dr. Julie Holland, MD, discusses in her book, Moody Bitches, medication doesn't need to be their long-term solution; within them women (and men) hold the key to transforming their lives and their perceived state of mind. There are many methods for increasing endorphins, natural hormones that improve mood, which can be incorporated into your daily routine and improve your outlook on life.

Our perception of stress as something we don't have any control over, or as a result of outside influences often prompts poor choices. We tend to respond to our stress in unhealthy ways such as the liberal use of drugs, cigarettes, alcohol, poor eating, overeating or becoming physically inactive. All of these vices damage the body in addition to the wear and tear of the stress itself. The use of these substances often leads you feeling even emptier, more depressed and despaired than you were before you used them. You can easily become stuck in a dead end situation going nowhere fast. You are no longer in control, your belief about stress is in charge.

You can lead a productive, fulfilling life and career without the need to endanger your health. Stress is a natural part of life. Stress can be both physical and mental. Sourced from how we process everyday pressures, each of us deals with stressors differently, some better than others. Your body is designed to work with a bit of stress and handle it. It is the overwhelming and chronic stress and anxiety that you want and need to learn how to shift, so you can manage your life and experience more joy. Left unchecked, as we just discussed, can lead to physical, emotional and behavioral disorders that can impact your health, vitality and peace of mind. It can wreak havoc on your personal and professional relationships. Identifying what is happening with your particular situation and being willing to do something about it is where the true

healing begins.

Awareness of the way stress, anxiety and grieving work allows you the ability to be more gentle and patient with yourself through your journey to healing. Once you understand the natural process that everyone goes through at the end of a relationship (no matter who ended the relationship), you can be more relaxed about what is happening to you. Utilizing the following suggested methods of taking control of your emotions begins to eliminate the amount of anxiety, fear, and stress.

You Can and You Will Thrive if
That is Your Deepest Desire!

Hopefully you know have more knowledge about the differences between stress and anxiety. It is time to take the next step toward healing and identify through the quizzes in your Thrive Anyway Clarity Journal. These simple tests are the third call to action that will help you identify your level of stress and provide insight on whether or not extra support may be helpful. The bonus materials we put together to support you in handling stress are also available for downloading and include 50 activities to help reduce levels of stress. If you haven't had a chance, these can be downloaded at:

www.thriveanywaybook.com/bonuses.

If you haven't already downloaded your Thrive
Anyway Clarity Journal Go Now To:
www.thriveanywaybook.com

Creating Your Happier Healthier You!

Change what you
have control over +
Accept what you
don't =
LESS STRESS

CHAPTER 4

Take Control of Your Stress Managment

As I've mentioned, stress is a natural part of your life, there is no getting rid of outside pressures, but there are ways in which you can shift how you perceive and react to them. In fact, that is all you have complete control over. You may find it hard to believe, but some stress is good for you. It comes bearing its gifts, like motivating you to do things you may normally avoid while in a relaxed state. It can give you enough adrenaline and courage to move forward on something when you might have normally hesitated. It might also prompt you to take action, speak up for yourself, or help someone else when you may have sat by passively.

Learning effective coping mechanisms for stress helps you to control it rather than allowing stress to manage and control your life. Building up your resiliency and strength to cope can be accomplished by learning certain tools and techniques for shifting your experience. Learning to make stress work FOR you and not AGAINST you is key. So how do you do that?

There are five key steps to managing your stress:

recognition

choice

perception shift

acceptance

action

recognition

When you begin to recognize the symptoms of stress, you can start to take charge of your process. While discerning that you are stressed is not always easy, you can be sure that anytime you are readjusting your life, stress is a result. When you begin a new job, end a relationship, start a relationship, give birth to a child, receive a promotion, speak in public, loss of a loved one - you get experience anxiety and stress.

Take notice and ask yourself: Where in my body am I feeling tense? Are you clenching your teeth, noticeably irritable, or not thinking clearly? Listen to your body and you will recognize these and other indicators such as sore muscles, shoulders pulled upward towards your ears, headaches, neck aches, furrowed brow, or inability to find humor. When you tune in and acknowledge that you are subconsciously choosing to be in a state of stress and decide that now is the time to do something different with it, you actually can.

choice

Once recognized–you get to identify the source and make a conscious choice about what you do to shift or decrease the stress. What changes are necessary, what beliefs need reinterpreting or what support do you need to help you reduce your stress? No one else can understand like you what the problem is, and you also know deep down what thought, perspective, belief or fear is fueling your body's stress response. Make a choice to shift these thoughts.

Close your eyes. Allow yourself to hear what you need at this very moment? What is the main fear or belief that is fueling your stress over this situation in your life? What thought can you let go or transform to move forward with ease? What support, structure or approach would be best to utilize to enable you to let go? Can you safely remove yourself from a disempowering situation? Could you take a break, walk or run? Do you need to talk to a friend, a professional or a loved one? Do you need to meditate, do some simple yoga or take a nap? Once you recognize what is fueling the stress reactors, you can choose to shift your interpretation.

perception shift

Transforming your viewpoint can begin to alter your experience and along with it, the intensity of your stress response. What belief is holding you, hostage? How likely is it to occur - percentage from 1-100? Where does it make you feel tense in your body? Once you've chosen which belief needs altering, can you grasp the gift or the positive impact of having experienced this point of view, fear or circumstance? Initially, seeing the gifts in it may not be easy, however, given some time, space, and a bit of humor, the gifts may be easier to recognize. For example, I believed it wasn't safe to let my former partners get too close emotionally, or they would hurt me, so I tended to pick partners that had difficulty expressing emotion and who kept an emotional distance. The gift was it protected my heart, but what I realized is, I no longer needed to do this. It isn't serving me now as I have developed healthy boundaries and no longer need protecting. I can have a partner who can discuss and express themselves and who I can open up to fully.

Even the most traumatic events come bearing helpful lessons. It is up to you to seek them out. Often when you do, it takes the intensity and sting out, allowing you to lessen the effects of the stress and putting you in charge of your experience. If appropriate, allow yourself to bring some humor to the situation and the belief that is fueling your stress. By shifting your emotional orientation to the underlying cause of your stress, it puts you in the driver seat.

After you become aware of the gifts of your initial fear, belief or commitment, ask yourself – "What is a more empowering mantra, belief or commitment that would move me forward? Similar to the mindset exercises in chapter 7, you may need to put some structure or support in place. Structures help remind you to keep repeating your new mantra, belief or commitment for three to four weeks until you fully shift. It often takes this long for it to sink into the brain and become a new pattern. For some, the shift is instant while others may need repetition to allow it to take hold.

Example:

Say your former partner is having a hard time with the end of your relationship and continues to text you, call you, follow you and send you things that you didn't request. Is it an attempt to hold on? Is it his way to convince you to come back? Avoid responsibility for her contribution to the end of your relationship? However you interpret it, it will give rise to your reaction. It is possible that you believe this behavior is irritating and immature. From those viewpoints, you begin to let it stress you out and cause you to get angry or frustrated. Possible you begin to worry that it won't ever end, that he will never move on, and you will be subjected to this forever. You could see it and receive the information in a whole different way; she is proving that you made the right decision for yourself. Each note, message, gesture, and gift are an affirmation that you were spot on about ending the relationship. You can celebrate and be happy.

Which belief empowers you towards healing? Does your new reaction stop his behavior? No. The behavior is about him and his needs. It honestly has nothing to do with you. Just be conscious of how you receive and process the events. You know it won't last forever and that simply observing it, not responding, is important. Privately acknowledge it as a sign that you made the best choice for yourself will move you towards experiencing less stress and more healing.

If the roles are in reverse, and you're the one that isn't letting go; think about the message you are sending. Recognize what your needs truly are so you can put an end to your behavior, setting yourself and the other person free.

acceptance

An acceptance-orientated approach again shifts the power over stress into your control. Fully accepting the situation or circumstance allows you to put yourself into a sustainable survival mode, moving you forward instead of keeping you stuck or in despair. If you are in acceptance, you are no longer a victim. You can actively begin to incorporate the tools, techniques, and structures that are going to support you in coping. Full acceptance enables you to move forward and experience less anger, grief, and stress.

Acceptance doesn't mean that other parties are not responsible for their role in the situation, or that you have to succumb to anything in particular. It just means that you see the situation clearly, you take responsibility for your part, and you now get to choose to move forward in a healthy and positive way. There is more about acceptance and strategies for acceptance in the upcoming chapters. When you are in acceptance of the situations causing stress, you are ready to move into the fifth and final step to managing your healing process - taking action.

action

Finally, you are clear how your perception and reaction to situations contribute to internalizing your stress. You've made a choice to bust the stress, and you can identify the beliefs that you choose to shift. You transform your perspective of the situation and accept it as it is. Now you can move powerfully into the final powerful actions you can do immediately and in future events that help you deal with the situation and reduce your stress in the healthiest way possible. Ask yourself what final actions do you need to take to move out of this stress? Now is the time to follow through with the final actions that will best support you. For example, if you transformed the meaning of the former partner's relentless reaching out to you (leaving texts and messages daily) as daily reminders you made the right decision - one further and a final action might be to change your number, so you don't receive the daily reminders any longer. It is the next step of action to move you forward and reduce the stress level.

The next chapter on phases of emotional grief will help you understand the natural process everyone goes through during a breakup and will lead you further down the road of gaining control of your life. One last thought in regards to handling your stress: focus on what is good, helpful and healing while giving yourself permission to allow any residual stress to melt away. Later in the book, there are other tools you can use to master transforming your stress and as a result, if applied, you will enjoy life more fully.

You Can and You Will Thrive if
That is Your Deepest Desire!

Taking control of your stress has never been easier once
you start implementing the five key steps of recognition,
choice, perception shift, acceptance and action. In your
Thrive Anyway Clarity Journal there is a chart to help you
track and move through the five steps for each stressor
you identified earlier in the journal. The fourth action step
is to take some time to work through some of the bigger
stressors you are currently experiencing and transforming
your relationship to them in order to move you forward in
your healing process. Know that if at anytime you are
working through your process, you can reach out through
social media for support or set up a one time free twenty
minute session with me at julieannabishop.com. If you
haven't joined our community page online, take a minute
to do so now: Facebook.com/thriveanyway.

If you haven't already downloaded your Thrive
Anyway Clarity Journal Go Now To:
www.thriveanywaybook.com

Creating Your Happier Healthier You!

Grief does
not change you ...
it *reveals* you.

-John Green
American Author

CHAPTER 5

Nine Emotional Stages of Grief and Loss

The end of a relationship brings about a tremendous amount of emotion. It is a grieving process similar to the grief that one experiences upon the death of a loved one. Each of the following emotional phases rises to the surface intermittently and sometimes simultaneously. Based on the classic work of Dr. Elisabeth Kübler-Ross in her book, On Death and Dying, I have expanded her five stages to nine. Her book has been helpful during my many losses, and I've often recommended it to others. Kübler-Ross's work depicted her observations of clients with a terminal illness and explored the emotions that were common among their experiences.

Knowledge about your process is the first step in dealing with grief. The known is much less stressful than the unknown. Therefore, understanding what is happening to you and the emotions that naturally occur during your process will help ease your mind as you are moving through it. Grieving is an inevitable part of your healing, and it is designed to help you naturally cope with your loss. The more familiar you are with how it works, the less stressful it will be and the quicker you will recover.

The nine emotional stages of broken-hearted grief are shock, denial, anger, bargaining, confusion, deep sadness (depression), fear, acceptance, and forgiveness. During a period after the end of your relationship, it can be quite maddening how randomly these pop-up. There is no set order, many can happen all at once, and you may skip past any one of them. The stages are not a formula. Become the observer of yourself and by that I mean pay attention to what you are thinking, feeling, and doing about these phases. In doing so, you will be able to move through them more easily. Once you understand how these phases of grief manifest in your life and have some tools to deal with them, you are better equipped to be gentle with yourself. Recognize these stages for what they are, a natural part of your process.

Note: It is important to realize that getting the support you need is key to taking care of yourself. Many people, I included, benefit from seeking the advice and counsel of professionals; therapists or coaches who are equipped to provide the necessary support and perspective to assist you in healing yourself. I've known many who resisted seeking help, and then after finally receiving it, found it to be amazingly freeing. Be completely honest with yourself if you would benefit.

> Just as the body
> goes into shock
> from a physical trauma,
> so does
> the human psyche
> go into shock
> after the impact
> of a major loss.
>
> - Anne Grant, poet

shock

Shock is nature's way of easing you gently into a new situation, allowing you to ease into a painful situation, so you don't suffer the full-blown devastation all at once. Shock may happen when the breakup blindsides you because on some level, you have been in denial about what was going in your relationship, or you had a big lack of communication. (There are signs things were headed south that we ignore, and once you have passed the point of shock and denial and had time to reflect, they become clearer.) It is also possible if you were the one to put an end to your relationship, to initially be in shock about your desire to leave. Your experience of denial or avoidance of the inevitable may have lasted for some time before making a decision. Some of us stay in a relationship far longer than may be healthy for us.

You are in the shock and denial phase when you experience thoughts and expressions such as "I had no idea he wasn't happy.", "How could she just throw away all those years we've been together?", "We just celebrated our anniversary and everything seemed fine!", "How can he do this to our family?!", or "I never thought I would feel this way, but leaving is the best choice for me."…etc.

Although this phase typically shows up in the beginning, shock can show up anytime during the process of getting over the end of your relationship. Shock can develop out of other people's reactions, stories they share because you are no longer together, things that your ex may say to others or confess that you weren't aware of before. It may be shocking to receive news that they had been unfaithful that was previously not on your radar. Shock occurs in reaction to how someone you've known for years suddenly and consistently speaks or acts out in ways you didn't know they were capable of displaying. (Actually, we are all capable of these actions and reactions given the proper circumstances, but that is another conversation.)

Fortunately, the shock is short-lived, it creates space for reality to set in, and it can make room for the transition between the other phases of grief. Shock is nothing to be ashamed of or to beat

yourself up over. It is completely a natural part of your grieving process.

So what can you learn from denial? What exactly do you do with it? How do you take the driver's seat when you find yourself here?

Here are some valuable tips:

1. First and foremost, you breathe. Slow deep inhales counting to four, holding for another count of four and releasing the exhale to the count of eight. Repeat this several times.

2. Express yourself and your dismay to a friend, another who is going through something similar, or just out loud to yourself in a mirror.

3. Write about it. I'm referring to writing a letter you may never send, writing in a notebook or journal, or keeping a secure online diary. Not somewhere public! I can't stress enough how Facebook pages or similar online social media venues are off-limits for spewing stuff about your ex. It's the number one place lawyers can grab slander to use against you in court.

4. On that note, blocking the person from your social media is a good thing if you are tempted to post negative information or if

they are posting negative information. You may have to block others that are close to them, but that is something you will have to decide for yourself.

5. Resist calling the ex. I know this can be difficult, but only connect over kids, lawyers, or the absolute musts. Texts are better and keep them neutral.

6. Give yourself time to get through the shock. A weekend away, a mini escape can do wonders to allow things to settle in. For some you will want to do this alone, for others, you may need to bring along a close friend.

7. Meditate. Guided meditation, stillness meditation, etc. can be helpful in this state of mind. There are 1,000 of ways to meditate, and it doesn't have to be lengthy. 5-10 minutes can do your mind and body wonders.

notes:

notes:

The thing about
denial is,
it doesn't feel like
denial
when it is going on.

- ,Georgina Kleege,
"Sight Unseen"

denial

Denial may show up more after the initial break up for the person that has been left because it is fresh. The "leaver" had already had her fair share of denial before making her decision and experienced less and less after she ended the relationship.

You can recognize your denial in thoughts and beliefs. Some examples include:

"If only I do this, he will come back,"

"She has done this before, she will come back again,"

"If we just go back to therapy we can work this all out,"

"He promises never to hit me again, I know he doesn't mean it,"

"Things aren't that bad, we can get through this," "He is a good man, he hasn't done anything wrong, why would I leave?"…etc.

There are times and places for denial, as it can be beneficial built in mechanism for transitioning. It gives space and time for one to adjust to a new situation. It covers your fear and keeps you safe from it. You may be so scared to see the truth; you lie to yourself. It is so powerful that it can keep you in a relationship much longer than is healthy for you, but eventually it catches up with you. You or your partner will come to a decision when you are ready. When the pain of staying is greater than the comfort of staying. The questions to ask yourself are - What is my denial hiding? What is my greatest fear?

It is normal for denial to pop up in the middle of your healing process. A time will come that you can see past it, look at the dynamics of your relationship, and determine it isn't healthy for you. You will recognize you both are better off. Healthier relationships await you. When you can confront the truth or accept your situation, you further your healing.

What can you do to support yourself during the emotional phase of denial? By its very nature, it is difficult actually to know you are in this, it is helpful to be ruthlessly honest with yourself. Try the following tips:

1. Does any of the before mentioned internal dialogue sound familiar to you? Identify the voice of denial in your life. If you can't, grab a friend that you know will be honest and ask them

where you might be in denial - then, ask yourself, if you knew what the actual truth of the matter at hand is, what would it be? Again, be gentle with yourself. You won't see anything you aren't equipped to handle.

2. If you do see something you weren't able to before, it is best to write it down. Determine what your ideal outcome would be and by when.

3. Make a list of action steps to take that will lead you to that desired outcome. When something comes up, and you aren't sure it is in alignment with your desired outcome, ask yourself - will this bring me closer to my goal or further? Take appropriate action and make choices that lead you forward.

notes:

> **Anger is an acid
> that can do more harm
> to the vessel
> in which it is stored
> than to anything
> on which it is poured.**
>
> - Mark Twain,
> *American Author*

anger

Anger is normal and appropriate to feel at the end of any relationship. Despite what you may have learned growing up, in school, church or society at large, anger can be a healthy emotion. Honestly, many things make you angry at the end of your relationship. Broken promises, unfulfilled dreams, and unmet expectations all give birth to anger. Feeling cast aside or not valued can fuel your inner rage. It is natural for you to feel this way. You can utilize healthy ways of expressing and releasing your anger so that you don't use inappropriate behavior. If not kept in check or expressed in a healthy manner, you may hurt yourself, your ex, or anyone else involved (children, family or new partner.)

Anger expressed may sound like, "I will never forgive him.", "I hate her so much.", "I want to make his life a living hell." etc. The important thing is not to act on your words. Find healthy venues in which to expel that angry energy. This anger will come up throughout your grieving and healing process and should lessen in time as you move further into the healing process. It usually winds down, if you can learn to express anger in healthy ways, by the time you find a place of forgiveness for your ex and yourself.

If your anger does get out of hand, and you find yourself ready to hurt yourself or someone else or the feelings don't subside after a long time, seek professional help. If your ex-partner hurts you, report it to the police, your therapist, your local abuse center and follow professional recommendations.

Anger is often a phase that gets people stuck. You know you are stuck when you can't seem to let it go, you aren't in control of it, and anger takes on a life of its own. This type of unchecked anger leads to resentment. If you hang onto your anger, blame, resentments or grudges for extended periods it is like you are carrying the individuals you feel wronged you around on your shoulders. They are still weighing you down and shackling your energy long after they have moved on. I think of what Deepak

Chopra shared regarding a quote by Nelson Mandela that deeply transformed his tendency to carry resentments. It goes something like this: "Holding onto resentment towards another is like drinking poison and expecting that he will die." A healthy way to handle anger and resentment is to acknowledge it, release it safely and find the gifts in the experience. You have a choice.

What are some healthy releases of anger? Try the following:

1. Get it out. Be sure to engage a family member, friend, therapist, or coach who can listen to your rants, your terrifying thoughts or feelings. Choose a person or persons who are not going to feel the need to give you any answers or who feel the need to defend your ex, but instead will allow you to express your real feelings.

2. Other methods of releasing your anger in a positive way include; intense physical exercise, participation in active sports, screaming into a pillow, yelling in your car with the windows up, beating a pillow, dancing it off, drumming, etc.

3. I had one workshop client that just couldn't tap into her anger even though the rest of the group recognized it was just below the surface waiting to explode. Some of the suggestions the group came up with for her were; Kickboxing, Zumba, smashing inexpensive or old plates, throwing rocks into the water and kneading the dough while pretending it was her ex.

notes:

> **In relationship, when does the art of compromise become compromising?**
>
> - Sarah Jessica Parker,
> American Actress

bargaining

Bargaining is possibly the most painful stage of the grieving process. It contains thoughts and feelings that may be different for everyone; regret, desperation, compassion, relief, hope, embarrassment to name a few. It can be truly demeaning for the one who was left, often frustrating for the "leaver", and mind numbing for the couple that makes this decision together. It is almost never successful in the long run. For example, a relationship that keeps breaking up every few weeks or months would be one stuck in bargaining. You may say or hear statements like, "I promise I will change this time.", "I will prove to you how much I love you; you'll see.", "I'll give him everything, and he will see how crazy it would be to leave me, he'll come running back.", "If only I do this, then.", and "let's go to couples therapy, it worked last time."

It is natural for you to engage in bargaining behavior. My former spouse and I repeated this phase for several years. It is a natural part of your grieving process. Sometimes, it can provide the time and space needed to make a healthy reconciliation from which the relationship may blossom. More often, however, it is borrowed time and just slows down the final decision making long enough to get you prepared for the inevitable. As you move through this stage, you can begin to make concrete decisions based on your deep inner needs, continue to heal, and get on with your life.

You can choose to continue the path of healing and find a meaningful, fulfilling and loving relationship with yourself. When you do put yourself first, you will realize that you deserve to be with who doesn't demand you to change or desire that you show up differently. A partner that values and respects you. Other potential partners will accept you fully as you are. Likewise, you will discover you can't expect others to change to fit your ideal and expectations. In healthy relationships, you accept your partner for exactly who he or she is, shortcomings and all. In a healthy relationship, neither of you is looking to fix or change anything about the other. You might support the other person if the other person desires to make changes in himself, but supporting and asking for change are two different things.

What can you do to navigate the emotional stage of bargaining? Again, this requires you to get truly honest with yourself and your expectations of the other person. The following are helpful questions that you can ask yourself and trust your initial knee-jerk response.

1. Are you expecting this person to show up differently or change in any way to please you and make the relationship work?

2. What expectations does this person ask of you? Changing because someone else wants you to will seldom work. Making changes because they are what you desire is much more successful. The motivation behind why you want to change is also valuable. Personal growth, your development, and healthier relationships are great self-motivators. Pleasing or living up to another person's expectations - not so fulfilling.

3. Run yourself and your former partner through the healthy partner filter at the end of this book. How does each of you add up as a healthy partner?

4. What qualities do you need to improve? You can't help the other person with their issues. Your job is to have a kick-ass relationship in the future is to become as healthy and whole as possible.

notes:

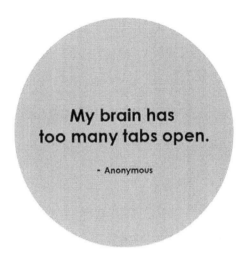

confusion

There will be multiple times throughout your breakup that your mind and state of being will find itself in the land of confusion. Everything seems out of focus, and you can't seem to get a handle on even the smallest of tasks. When forgetfulness settles in, you may leave the stove or oven on or forget what the day of the week is or not be able to think of a simple word. Remember that this isn't your normal state of being. DON'T PANIC. You have not lost your mind, and most likely you are not suffering from early dementia. You are experiencing a stress-induced state of confusion. I can recall clearly the day I put a pint of Ben and Jerry's ice cream into the refrigerator, and one of my friends left his car running all day four months after his break up. I have had clients who have forgotten things - where they have parked at the mall, to pick their child up after school, and to go to appointments - during the confusion phase.

While it is annoying, it is yet another coping mechanism that occurs after a loss. It's perfectly natural. For those of you who are mothers, I would compare it to pregnancy brain. Confusion places you in the pleasantly unaware and non-tuned-in category, so you aren't fully experiencing all the pain at once. This phase can make you feel like you are in a stupor, a malaise or a cloud of daydreams. Your mind wanders. You may be running at times on autopilot or so caught up in running what went wrong, what could you have done differently or various other scenarios over and over in your mind. It just means you simply aren't present or paying attention to what requires your focus. While being in this frame of mind does allow you to escape, it can also be very frustrating for those of you that are used to being in control, responsible or on time.

Possibly, you have just gone through shock and denial, landing in a state of confusion as to how your relationship even ended. You are not likely to get the answers you seek from your ex. In fact, it is highly suggested, once again, that you refrain from having contact with your ex for anything, except meeting with your attorneys or mediator to pan out the details. If you have joint custody, you will also need to communicate in arranging or discussing matters that pertain to your children and pets. Keep it factual, non-emotional, neutral and to the bare necessities. Many of my clients and myself found it best to use texts and emails for these interactions, especially when talking ends up in arguing. Attempting to get clarity from your former partner's explanation as to why they are no longer into you typically leads to only more confusion.

Since there is not much in the way of accomplishing things during this phase, it can be particularly frustrating if you are typically very productive. That was my biggest complaint about my confusion because honestly, being timely and remembering my schedule are not my greatest strengths. Being creative and producing, however, was/is a huge part of my way of being. It was a challenge to be gentle and patient with this phase. I had to learn to break things down into simple steps, utilize a reminder system to ease the frustration. What do you need to do for yourself to move as smoothly as possible during this stage? How do you best support yourself? Try some of the following tips:

1. Don't beat yourself up for your confusion. Learn to be gentle with yourself as well as to have patience.

2. Create reminders, use alarm reminders on your computer and phone and ask colleagues to help remind you.

3. At your work, surround yourself with others whom you can enroll to help keep you on task or delegate responsibilities to lighten your load.

4. Do not be afraid to reach out to your family and friends (your children included). If it's difficult, ask yourself, "Would I do this for them?" It is an effective way to learn the gift of receiving and honestly, your friends, family, and children want to feel useful because most likely they feel helpless to help your broken heart otherwise.

5. And be kind to yourself, don't schedule things that need decisive action, deadlines or brain power if you can help it.

notes:

notes:

I never guessed
I could cry
so hard that
my face hurt.

- Vernor Vinge,
"A Fire Upon The Deep"

deep sadness

Deep sadness is a type of depression is sorrow and anger aimed inwardly. The phase of deep sadness is not to be confused with clinical depression that can also come from the loss of a significant relationship; we will discuss that type of depression later. Natural sadness occurs during the grieving and healing process. In this regular form of depression, you recognize you're sad, you allow yourself to cry, give yourself space to feel your feelings, or to have an "off" day. You may even temporarily wallow in self-pity, indulge briefly in unworthiness, or slightly beat yourself up on the inside, but you don't stay here for extended periods of time. The gift of this stage is it allows you to process and release your grief. You aren't holding it in; you are expressing your emotion one way or another through tears, talking, or thinking about your loss.

At a certain point, you do want to consider what your sadness is making you believe about yourself. You look for the belief or the meaning you make about why you are sad, and you can begin to work to let it go. To do so, you must shift your interpretation and create a belief that is more empowering so you can move through the sadness and not get stuck in it.

Your support structure– friends, family members, therapist or coach– are essential during these times. Prayer and meditation can also help you get through these moments. You may hear thoughts like: "I hate myself.", "This is all my fault, if only...", "I don't matter.", "I am damaged, who will ever want me?" etc. Those are all beliefs that can change and you don't have to buy into them as a "fact/truth" or a "definition" of who you are. Acknowledge what thought or belief has you feeling horrible and re-frame it. For example, "I don't matter" can be re-framed to be, "Because I am alive, I have value or else I wouldn't exist", "I choose to matter for myself", and "My family believes that I matter." Which belief do you think will empower you? What will move you forward and heal? It is your choice.

Depression is different than deep sadness. How to tell the difference? What you have to watch for is sinking into a sea of these feelings. Observe if you are dropping into a pit of despair that you don't feel you can climb out of alone. Look for thoughts on a consistent basis of wanting to harm yourself or not go on. If any of these are the case, it is time to reach out and get more help. If this describes you, you could be suffering from clinical depression. It is important for you to seek out the help of a medical professional, preferably a doctor or a therapist who specialize in helping people identify the underlying issues creating the depression. If you can identify them, you can transform the beliefs and heal. These professionals will have recommendations for diet, supplements and medications that can assist you in your process. Losing someone in your life is not worth giving up on your own, so if you feel suicidal, call the National Suicide Hotline at 1-800-273-8255. The greatest satisfaction you can have regarding someone who you feel has hurt you to heal your own heart. MOVE ON, become an authentic, complete and whole person— live a full, kick-ass and spectacular life.

What can you do to move through deep sadness as smoothly as possible?

In addition to the simple actions above, you can:

1. Get good night's sleep, at least 7-8 consecutive hours.

2. Exercise, walk and being active naturally releases endorphins as does having a friend to hold/cuddle you.

3. Don't bottle up your feelings, instead share them with someone who can console or counsel you.

4. Invest time, energy and money toward your well-being to cultivate true inner happiness - not the kind of temporary joy that is reliant on outside circumstances, people or other external factors.

5. Find ways to serve others - give of yourself.

6. Involve yourself in projects you enjoy.

7. Create a one-year-from-today goal for yourself and begin taking action each week to make it happen.

notes:

notes:

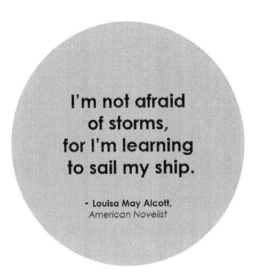

I'm not afraid
of storms,
for I'm learning
to sail my ship.

- Louisa May Alcott,
American Novelist

fear

When you are going through a major break up, fear and worry often lurk in your daily thoughts and actions. "How will I support myself? And my family?", "Will my children be permanently damaged?", "Do I have enough courage to see this through?", "Will I ever be loved again?" so on and so forth ... the fear tape in your mind seems to be caught in a loop and rambles on.

Fear can be a useful emotion that keeps you out of harm's way. It is a primal human response that alerts you when you are in danger and prompts quick action to avoid pain. However, at times when fear shifts into overdrive, it gets your nervous system running in circles. Subconsciously, it begins to impact your decisions, choices and ability to take action as if you were on autopilot and fear is in the driver's seat.

Fear completely normal while going through any traumatic life transition. When fear is in control, the effects are less than empowering. When fear robs you of the life you desire, it renders you powerless. Fear freezes you from making any forward momentum, steals your joy, makes you shrink. It can often drive you to invisibility and seals your lips shut when you need to speak up the most. If you are stuck in fear, you can guarantee that your life is unfulfilled. Taking back control is essential.

The first step to gaining control is the same as when you are taking back control of your stress, recognition. You must first recognize the voice of fear within your head. How do you experience fear and what does fear say to you? Internal chatter in your mind; loops of self-criticism, monotonous monologs of dis-empowering self-doubt, lack, worry, what ifs? It can be so continuous and loud; you start believing it as truth. You can confuse the voice of fear with certainty. What does your fear say to you? What do other's fears and worry say to you? The only way to deal with fear is to face it. Debunk the fear with the truth. If you don't, you allow it to gain strength, and it becomes a subconscious determinant to what you can have and cannot have in your life. Unchecked fear is like a tsunami washing over your entire life and drowning out all

possibilities of joy. You can break the fear cycle and take
back control.

As I already mentioned, the first step is being mindful that fear has a hold of you. Recognizing the voice of fear begins to weaken its hold. Take notice of this emotion and how it is currently impacting your personal experience. Do you lay awake at night, reviewing over and over the worst outcomes? When you do, ask yourself what is the percentage of my fear coming true? Is it 90% or 10%? Eliminate the many worries that have little probability of coming true and are taking up too much of your energy.

I am an Integrative Courage Coach trained and certified by Debbie Ford, an amazing spiritual teacher, leader and human being that passed in 2013. Before my certification, I was so fortunate to volunteer to be one of her coaching clients as she wrote her ninth best seller, Courage: Overcoming Fear and Igniting Self-Confidence. In that book, she shares, "Fear can make us choose what we believe will keep us safe when the opposite is true. It can make us think that we can't do it, we are wrong, the cost is too high, the path ahead too difficult. Fear disguises itself with the voice of certainty, filling us with worry, doubt, and even dread. Fear is a very real emotion that can render us powerless." It was this experience with Debbie, which I was able to understand and get very real with the strength fear had over me. Up until that point, regardless of the years of personal growth and development

I had been through, it was the voice of fear that kept me from facing my denial about the unhealthy partnership I had with my now former husband. It kept me in a relationship that reflected my old belief system of self-loathing which fed my self-doubting fear that I couldn't make it on my own.

I also learned from Debbie that by uncovering, understanding and ultimately embracing fear through finding its gifts - I was naturally launched into courage, confidence, and self-esteem. You can transform your fears into catalysts for courage. Courage comes from a deep place within. With it, you can face your fears and move through them one at a time. You aren't trying to get rid of the fear; you are working to transform your relationship to it; shift your perspective of it, take away its power over you, and use it to make choices that are empowering for you as well as those you love.

Taking back control of fear can begin with the following exercise:

1. In a journal or in the note section to follow - Draw five columns. In the first column list out all of the biggest fears, that keep you up at night or seem to repeat frequently. If you can't think of any, close your eyes, take a few deep breaths and ask yourself, "What are my biggest fears right now?"

2. In the second column, write down on a scale of 1% - 100% the likelihood that your fear will come true.

3. In the third column write down what believing this fear protects you from; does it keep your heart safe? Keep you from feeling something? Is it more comfortable to just keep things as they are? What does your fear give you? (if you can't think of any, try closing your eyes, take a few deep breaths and ask yourself again)

4. Write down in the fourth column, what you would have more of in your life if you were in control of this fear and it wasn't controlling your actions? Energy, time, productiveness, joy, etc.?

5. In the fifth and final column: What action could you take, new belief could you adopt, or a new interpretation of this fear that will empower you?

Note: It can be very helpful to journal about what you discover and to post the new belief or interpretation on an index card, hanging it where you will see it every day for the next month and can repeat it to yourself often. If you continue to struggle with your fears, I highly recommend diving further into the journey of courage in Debbie Ford's book, *"Courage: Overcoming Fear and Igniting Self-Confidence"*.

notes:

> There is nothing
> either good or bad,
> but thinking
> makes it so.
>
> - William Shakespeare,
> *Hamlet*

acceptance

The stage of acceptance, or phase as I prefer to think of it, is one of the most liberating of the grieving process. Even though there will be periods and levels of acceptance that you will reach throughout your journey of grief, when you land fully in true acceptance healing has begun. In fact without acceptance, forgiveness and full recovery aren't possible.

Acceptance is also a treasured tool for stress reduction. It is a state of mind you reach when you recognize and acknowledge your situation for what it is and what it isn't. Allow your situation to be as it is without the need to make it any different. When you choose acceptance (and it is a conscious choice) for a situation, person or event, immediately you begin to relax, and suddenly, you are in control of your reactions.

Acceptance can be difficult, painful, beautiful and exhilarating. There is no telling what it will hold for you, but you will experience it. You will have moments of clarity amidst your process. Steadily you will gain acceptance for the completion of your relationship. You will eventually be able if you choose, to fully accept your responsibility for your part in the breakdown of your relationship. You will realize the lessons you've learned because of it, and know that you are healthier without the relationship. You will know it is complete. When you can be with all of that—you are ready to move onward.

Ideally, if you are in a divorce situation, you will wait to negotiate important terms when you both are in a place of acceptance. You will make better choices and decisions for yourselves and your children if you have any. How long it takes to reach full acceptance varies for every person. In a divorce, it is often a two to three-year process depending on the parties involved and how long they worked on their issues before their split. That being the case, it isn't always practical to defer your negotiations.

Acceptance on all levels and of all parties is your key to freedom in many respects. It does take time however and the more self-accepting you can be in the process, the quicker your ability to heal. When you are in acceptance, you are no longer in a blame and judgment mode (making either yourself or your former partner wrong), and you are no longer in denial. When you are in acceptance, you are understanding, compassionate, and patient. You are ready for forgiveness.

What can you do to support yourself in becoming accepting of your situation and those involved? Follow these tips:

1. Make your experience meaningful. Find the gift or lesson by exploring the possibilities and opportunities that can come from the end of this relationship.

2. Adopt a positive mindset vs. negative mindset (see the section on taming your negative mindset for exercises).

3. Recognize you can't change or control the past and let go of trying to. See it for what it is. You don't have to agree with how it played out, but you can accept that it truly over.

4. Focus on what you want for yourself moving forward and let go of the expectations you had for this person and that relationship.

5. Do something ceremonial to cut the ties that bound you to this partner. You can either do this with others or on your own. With

others, you can take a string or rope that represents your energetic cord connection to the other person. Have two friends hold it while you cut it. If you are on your own, imagine a golden cord going from your heart to the heart of the person you are letting go. Visualize a beautiful knife or scissors and you cut the cord. Then visualize it disconnecting from both of you and dissolving into thin air.

notes:

notes:

True forgiveness is
when you can say,
"Thank you
for that experience."

- Oprah Winfrey,
American Queen of Media

forgiveness

The MOST LIBERATING phase on your road to recovery is without a doubt forgiveness. Forgiveness of others and yourself is the key to liberation, freedom, and peace. I can imagine that when you read this if you aren't anywhere close to this phase, it may seem repulsive, or you may wish to skip all the others stages to land here. But grief is a process and getting to your broken heart takes time.

The most common misconception about forgiveness is that it lets someone walk free from any responsibility for their part in causing pain in the first place. Forgiveness is not about the other person; it's about your freedom. The last thing that would be beneficial to you is to carry around resentments toward another human being.

Do you think they need, want or care about your forgiveness? While some might, most aren't interested or concerned. Holding it back to punish another person never works, in fact much like the poison we mentioned earlier, it only hurts you. I repeat, it only hurts you.

As stated in the beginning, I believed my mother's death was due partially to her inability to cope with the stress and emotions that came from her separation from my father. Inadvertently, I harbored a great deal of anger, judgment and blame towards my dad as a teenager. After a time, and with only having one parent left, those thoughts and feelings were buried. I wasn't even consciously aware they existed as they lay underneath the surface, stuffed down and undealt with for twenty-two years until, during a guided meditation aimed at bringing up someone I most needed to forgive to move forward in my life, my father appeared in my visualization. In real life, he didn't even know he needed forgiveness, so my process was not about him. At thirty-eight years old, I was able to release this pent up anger, judgment and blame that took an enormous emotional and psychological weight off my back I didn't even know I was carrying. I took him out one day and confessed my process. He grabbed my hands, with that twinkle in his eye, told me he was glad I worked through it and he loved me. I believe I'm the one that benefited the most.

So I highly recommend you don't carry this weight, or suppress your anger, judgment, and blame against your former partner, as it will impact what you can have or create in your relationships moving forward. In fact, you may even repeat the same scenario with the next partner. It is best to deal with it now when you are ready. The best way to deal with anger is to allow yourself to see it, feel it and express it in a healthy manner.

The following are helpful exercises when working on acceptance and forgiveness of self or others. The first is an exercise provided by my friend and mentor, Clifford B. Edwards from his enlightened book, The Forgiveness Handbook: A Simple Guide to Freedom of the Mind and Heart. You can find out more at www.theforgivenesshandbook.com

1. Write a forgiveness letter to the person that hurt you. Write out anything and everything that you would want to say to them to express your feelings, release your judgments, to reclaim your responsibility and power, and to forgive, let go of the baggage and be clean, clear and complete with them. Remember, this is for you, this note does not need to be seen by anyone or sent to the individual. More resources available at www.forgivenessclub.com. In all the letters I've written when doing this work, I prefer to burn them for me to feel complete. Ask yourself what would be the best method to deal with yours? Trust your answer.

2. Take it one step beyond Cliff's recommendation and write a letter from a place of compassion, from a "bigger" point of view, a "divine" point of view, as if this situation was exactly what needed to happen for you to grow and the other person to expand as well. From this spiritual perspective, imagine you secretly agreed before you were born to have this relationship—you both arranged how it would end this particular way, no matter how bad it seemed to be when it finished, so you could both learn something and evolve.

Note: This second letter possesses the ability to allow you to move on and heal with a great deal of enlightenment and freedom. I know I found it useful to do the exercise first with my former spouse in mind and then to repeat it a second time with myself. Self-forgiveness is equally important. I physically felt much lighter and more energetic about moving forward with my life through self-forgiveness.

3. Create a self-forgiveness and acknowledgment journal. At the end of the day, write down one thing you did that day that you judged as not quite perfect, or you were hard on yourself for as well as one thing you were proud of doing. Forgive yourself for it by finding either some positive outcome that may have happened as a result or by acknowledging that everyone makes mistakes. Encourage yourself with positive thought such as "there will be an opportunity to make new choices the next time." Take time to acknowledge what did go well.

notes:

notes:

stages of grief summary

You may find yourself accepting the end of your relationship one minute, bargaining to get back together the next, and yet another moment being angry and blaming your ex for everything under the sun. One second you are sulking and kicking yourself for your situation and the next you're in acceptance that it's truly for the best. This process is completely maddening yet natural experience.

Often people think they are over their grieving process only to run into a mutual friend of their former partner's or to have some memory of the past triggered which then sets them back– again, it is a natural part of the process. I've been there more than once, and you may visit it a few times too. The good news is that the grieving process will eventually run its course, you will heal and can choose to move on to enjoy a fulfilling life. Isn't that liberating, you have a choice? What is your choice going to be? You are most likely reading this right now because on some level you are choosing to cope, heal and live your life more fully.

You Can and You Will Thrive if
That is Your Deepest Desire!

Wow, you've made it through half of Thrive Anyway!
I hope you have been taking advantage of the Thrive
Anyway Clarity Journal. Now is the time to identify
where you are in your grieving process. If you haven't
already, go back through the stages of grief you most
identify with right now to answer the corresponding
questions in your journal. Understanding where you
are and what you can do to move through the stage
you're in is vital to your healing. Sometimes, the
healing takes place in giving yourself permission to
just be with what is, observe it, don't judge it, and
allow yourself time to process it. You've got this!

If you haven't already downloaded your Thrive
Anyway Clarity Journal Go Now To:
www.thriveanywaybook.com

Creating Your Happier Healthier You!

Good Fences make good neighbors.

- Rober Frost,
American Poet

CHAPTER 6

Setting Healthy Boundaries

Healthy boundaries are not something many of us instinctively know how to set, more often it is a learned skill. Setting healthy boundaries is a means of self-respect and compassion. They benefit every relationship in your life. Somewhere along the line, however, life events and emotional wounds happen, impairing your ability to speak up for yourself. You might find yourself saying yes when you want to say no. Although this makes defining and setting clear boundaries more difficult, you can learn to set them. In fact for your freedom and peace-of-mind, they are essential.

I began realizing the importance of boundary work after leading a therapeutic recreation program in a nursing home with residents diagnosed with dementia. After a long day's work, I would leave tense, drained, exhausted and overwhelmed. I was caught up in the individual lives of those I served - their drama, needs, and well-being - so much so, I couldn't let it go when I went home. In other areas of my life, the same thing was happening: the edges of where I ended and family, intimate partners and friends began were blurred. It would leave me unsure of who I was, powerless, unfocused, consumed by other's dramas and unheard. I was not setting healthy personal boundaries; being overly responsible for others and their business. The vital information I was missing; I didn't realize that these individuals never asked me to take their stuff on, worry about them or stress over their needs. My personal and professional lives suffered; I wasn't taking care of myself and my resentments were growing. I knew this way of being wasn't working and that I was the one that needed to change. My supervisor at the time noticed the dilemma as she had experienced the same situation earlier in her career. She gently suggested I determine what my boundaries are and find time to recharge myself in my free time. Self-care was a whole new concept to me as it is not the example I learned growing up. I wasn't even clear on what she meant. Nevertheless, my quest for setting healthy boundaries began.

What I've learned is that getting used to setting healthy boundaries takes time and practice. I started identifying people in my family and past whom I spent a great deal time and energy worrying over.

I began to visualize each person and determine what I was taking on of their "stuff." In my visualization, I would picture myself with a big sack of their struggles that I then took off my back and handed back to them, saying "I am sorry I felt I needed to carry this for you and didn't trust you to do it on your own. I am now letting it go and returning it back to you where it belongs. Thank you, I love you, and I trust that you know how to handle your stuff." Once I did this for family, past and present, I reviewed all my past and current clients, friends, and lovers. Letting go and releasing myself from the self-imposed excessive worry removed an enormous weight from my shoulders. I've taught this process to clients and get great feedback that they too, feel freedom from their self-induced burden of over responsibility for others. To maintain this freedom, do this process as a weekly practice in which you can ask yourself "whose stuff am I carrying now and do I need to give anything back to anyone?" It is good practice to repeat until you can identify exactly when you are becoming responsible for someone's business, and you stop yourself at the moment before "taking it on."

At first, you may feel a bit selfish or embarrassed to set a boundary. I recommend you do it despite your reluctance and tell yourself that you value your needs and are supporting the other person in taking responsibility for their needs as well. In fact, self-value is healthy self-care. Truly loving another is accepting them fully as they are and respecting them in taking care of their needs.

There may be people who are happy you don't have boundaries so that they can let you do the worrying for them or in some cases - manipulate, control and dominate you. Be clear, firm and direct when you are establishing a boundary. When your boundaries get breached, it is most frequently because they are weak, unguarded or unclear. If this is the case, you will let in all sorts of stuff that isn't yours as well as give away your personal energy. It is often an unconscious leak or exchange, so it's important to pay attention to whom upsets you, drains you or with whom you feel you lose yourself. Notice how it feels in your body and your mind. If it feels off, wrong or uncomfortable those are great indicators you need a boundary. This discomfort will be your internal cue to establish or re-establish a healthy boundary.

Give yourself permission to let go of relationships that are toxic - toxic relationships are a form of abuse and manipulation. Sometimes you just need to hear it is okay to end the relationship. Guess who is the expert to give you that permission? It's you. Toxicity is about the other person's needs or wounds and has nothing to do with you. It isn't yours to take on, and this individual will have an extremely difficult time letting go of you. The clearer you are and the firmer your boundaries, the better.

In my life, I had a friend in college that had very poor boundaries. At first, it didn't seem to be an issue, but when I started to date, he didn't do well with the men in my life. He drove three hours to my hometown to interrupt the weekend I was introducing my new boyfriend to my family. It was always clear that this person and I were just friends. He was almost three times my age and not once did our interactions ever signify a romance. He began to stalk me once I returned to school. He called frequently. I had to end our relationship, change my phone lines and keep my numbers non-published for many years. I struggled with taking such drastic measures, but it continued over a year despite all my efforts. This was a valuable lesson in setting up healthy boundaries and maintaining them.

I've had some clients who have struggled around this in regards to a close relative such as a parent or a sibling. If this person is unable to stop treating you abusively or in a toxic manner, you can make a conscious choice to limit your interactions or to eliminate your interactions all together as needed for your sanity. You can choose whether or not to engage in difficult conversations, whether or not you respond to negative comments or condescension. You are in charge of your response and level of boundary necessary for your health and well-being.

Healthy boundaries are necessary for healthy relationships. Many people struggle with creating and maintaining healthy boundaries, yet it is essential for your sanity and was as the sanity of those you are in a relationship with; your ex, your lover, children, parents, siblings, relatives, friends, colleagues, acquaintances and even strangers. Your boundaries will be different from individual to individual and will depend on their maturity level with their borders. You can't change theirs; you only have control over your own. Your personal limits may need to change when it comes to friends and family of your former partner. Just how that unfolds may take time and communication between each. Their comfort levels may shift with the dynamic change, so honest, open communication is best.

You Can and You Will Thrive if
That is Your Deepest Desire!

Healthy boundaries alone can transform your life and create a happy, healthier you. If all you did as a result of this book was instill better boundaries in your life, you will notice a huge difference in your energy level, your amount of joy and better interactions with others. Your sixth action step is to take some time to fill out the boundary chart in your Thrive Anyway Clarity Journal. Be sure to share your findings and insights on the community page at:

www.facebook.com/thriveanyway.

If you haven't already downloaded your Thrive Anyway Clarity Journal Go Now To:
www.thriveanywaybook.com

Creating Your Happier Healthier You!

If you get
the inside right,
the outside will
fall into place.

- Eckhart Tolle,
Spiritual Teacher

CHAPTER 7

Tame Your Mindsets

There are three mindsets that you may be engaging in that can impede your healing process and stop you from enjoying a less traumatic recovery:

1. Negative Mindset

2. Fault--Focused Mindset

3. People-Pleasing Mindset

Recognizing these barriers can be a stellar first step toward managing problems in relationships that create stress. Taming and transforming your perspective of these behaviors can go far in managing your stress and lead to healthier relationships moving forward.

The trouble is; most of us can't easily switch our behavior by the mere discovery of it. I have personally struggled with each of the following mindsets and have found great techniques that have put me on the road to recovery. That said, I revisit these exercises when I find myself needing a refresher because we all dip into these mindsets from time to time. What we want to avoid is dwelling in them without realizing that this is where our minds are defaulting.

Your mindset is a habit, a deep groove, or a pattern that, according to bestselling author and spiritual growth leader–Debbie Ford, was developed in the early years of your life and operates in your subconscious until you are ready to shift them. It is my belief that some of these mindsets or beliefs may have been experienced in past lifetimes or at the very least, were passed down through your ancestors. Recognizing your mindset default is the first step. Making peace with it and yourself is your second step. Creating a new behavior is the third step. It can take 21 to 30 days of mindfully engaging in the new mindset to make it a habit, but it is well worth the effort. All three mindsets can be intertwined, can be altered independently or simultaneously.

Debbie also shares in her work that when you can accept all parts of yourself, knowing that each of them isn't negative or positive, good or bad, you can truly be whole. Each trait has a purpose and comes bearing a gift. In the following exercises, you are engaging in the process of becoming more and more self-realized, healthy, and self-loving. You are safe to be the person you authentically are, and others will respect you for it. Don't give away your power by hiding from parts of yourself that make you uncomfortable. Instead, continue to reclaim the traits you desire in your life one by one and start finding the gifts in the characteristics you don't like or are afraid of - one by one. You can repeat any of the following mindset exercises as often as needed - they will continue to transform your experience of yourself.

negative mindset

The first is obsessive negativity. When you are obsessively negative, especially during a breakup, it means that you have a tendency toward using a "negative" viewpoint about people, places, situations, and things in your life. It is going to make for a very stressful time, long grieving period and a slow healing process. For example, you may say things like: "I can't do this!" or "No one understands!" or "Nothing ever works!" You may be somewhat aware that you chose this negative perspective from time to time, but you often default here unconsciously. Essentially you have what is commonly called a negative mindset.

Believe it or not, your life will reflect back this negative thinking over and over again validating to your mind and ego that your negative belief is true. It will be all you can see because you are filtering your life through a negative lens. This negative mindset holds you back from knowing what it's like to view life from a positive perspective. It is keeping you stuck in relationships that don't support you and limiting your experience of the world. This exercise can help you shift your perspective and create new neural grooves in your brain for transforming your mindset.

Taming Your Negative Mindset Exercise:

(I recommend this exercise even if you think you don't have a negative mindset, we all have negative behaviors that hold us back from time to time.)

1. Close your eyes and for 30 seconds invite all of the negative feelings, thoughts, or sayings into your awareness—the negative things you hear yourself often say about your life, yourself and your current situation. Open your eyes. When ready, jot down your list.

2. Read your list out loud. Close your eyes. Take a deep breath. Ask yourself which one of these statements stresses me out and drains my energy the most? Write out the one negative statement that stood out. List at least four negative experiences from your life that validate this statement and proves to you that it is true.

3. For each of these four negative examples in your life, think of one positive thing you can learn from or that came as a result of these experiences. (If you are struggling, see the example given at the end of the exercise.)

4. Close your eyes. Envision a new statement that is contrary to the statement that stood out. What new mantra would be more empowering, energetic and less stressful? When you have one, write it down.

5. Write this statement and place it somewhere that you can view it each day. When you see it, read it to yourself or out loud. Using the combination of a physical action such as pinching your ear, snapping your fingers, or tapping your knee as you repeat this new statement to yourself. Do this at least twice a day for the next 21-30 days.

Note: Repeating this statement and accompanying gesture as often as possible allows you to create a new habit, behavior, and ultimately new experiences. You are creating new neural pathways in your brain. These new experiences will begin to show up to reflect this new empowering statement. If the old way brought negative experiences to validate it, no less is true if you apply a new positive mindset. You will know it is working when you start seeing that the events in your life reflect it to be true.

An example of this exercise:

1. Negative thought: No one ever supports me.

2. Experience from my life to prove it true: My boyfriend did not want me to go back to school. He consistently gave me a difficult time about it. Often attempting to keep me from attending my classes. He didn't value it or me. He actually told me it was a waste of my time; I should be working full time to pay my bills instead.

3. Positive lessons learned: His not supporting me drove me to work harder. Because of the experience, I am more self-reliant and independent. I learned not to need his approval or support while learning to support and validate myself.

4. Positive thought: I support myself, I have all I need to succeed.

5. Event to reflect the new belief, behavior, thought: I graduated with ease, do work I love and pay my bills. (without that boyfriend)

fault-focused mindset

Another stress creator during a breakup is the fault-focused mindset: engaging in obsessive comparison to others, focusing on all your perceived faults and devaluing what you uniquely have to offer. Fault-focused mindset is a close cousin to the negative mindset. However, it shows up a little differently and is rooted in insecurity and low self-esteem. It can be a form of perfectionism (holding yourself to unrealistic standards). The fault-focused mindset can be impacted and bolstered by those you are influenced by, such as a fault-focused ex-partner, friend, or parent.

How often do you inwardly compare yourself to the others at your office, at the gym, or when you are at the beach? Maybe you compare yourself and your life to your close friends. Most of us have been there, done that, right?! However, when you regularly engage in these behaviors, such as comparison, putting yourself down because you don't measure up or being jealous of what your friend just achieved, you are essentially engaging in emotionally abusing yourself. Through your beliefs that you can never live up to someone else's beauty, intelligence, style or whatever it is that you tell yourself they have, and you don't, you are putting unnecessary pressure and stress on yourself. This form of self-abuse does not empower you in any way, shape or form.

Ever heard from a friend that you are "your worst critic?" Ever find that nothing is ever good enough, especially you? You may find yourself making statements such as, "I will never be that pretty.", or "I'm such a failure!" or "I could never do that.", "Why can't I be more like him.", "I'm not good enough.", or "Something is wrong with me."

Negative thinking can even show up in the form of always finding fault with others and the events in your life. That may sound like, "She thinks she's so great, I could do that better than her." Again, this behavior may be totally beyond your awareness, but it interferes with your ability to love yourself or others. Don't you want to feel good about yourself? How are you ever going to get that relationship you'll love without first knowing how to love yourself for who you are? I am not referring to being self-absorbed, selfish, vain, or a narcissist. I am talking about self-value, self-care, and self-respect. No one is going to do that for you, and if you want someone to love and value you as you are, you need to be able to do it first.

Transforming Your Fault Focused Mindset Exercise:

You will need a journal, notebook or pad of paper and a pen before you begin this exercise. Write it in this book if need be, just be sure to write your answers somewhere. This exercise can be repeated as many times as needed. I learned this in my training to become an Certified Integrative Coach™ from The Ford Institute of Transformational Training. The following is an abbreviated version of a much deeper process that you can experience when you work with me or another integrative coach directly.

1. Close your eyes and for about 30 seconds allow yourself to visualize someone who you compare yourself with often, that you feel you don't live up to or believe you fall short of being like - could be a sibling, parent, friend, boss, public figure, or Hollywood star.

2. Then allow yourself to hear what mind-chatter or judgments you use when comparing yourself to this person. Open your eyes. Take a few moments to write about the person and your mind-chatter of why you fall short or why you could never be what you perceive them to be. Feel free to add some if more thoughts come to you while you begin writing the first few.

3. Now close your eyes again, visualize this person again, along with the comparison and allow yourself to identify the traits that you believe this person has and you don't. (Example traits: Intelligent, wise, compassionate, spiritual, etc.)

4. Select one of this person's trait you desire to express the most. We all have the capacity to exhibit any characteristic that we recognize in others. Close your eyes. Ask yourself what would be four actions could you take to support yourself in developing and expressing this aspect in your life? Write down the desired traits

and an action step next to each one on what you are going to do to help yourself embody that attribute over the next 21 to 30 days.

5. Once again, close your eyes and for the next 30 seconds, allow yourself to hear all the types of traits and actions you constantly criticize yourself for or dislike about yourself. Pick four and list in your journal. Which one of your traits irritates and stresses you the most? Circle it.

6. Brainstorm the gift or benefit of having each this trait. Is there any way having this trait helps you? (see examples below) How might it be used in a positive or purposeful way?

7. Acknowledge the gifts from the traits you found at fault. Does it feel less repulsive now that it you can see the potential use or need of these characteristic? If you can't find anything good about the trait, post it on the Thrive Anyway Facebook page.

8. Make an inventory of all the attributes that you enjoy about yourself or that you think your friends and others see in you that they enjoy. Read through this list out loud and slowly to yourself in a mirror. Acknowledge yourself for each characteristic and allow

An example of this exercise:

1. Positive trait: Courageous.

2. Actions one could take to be more courageous: Learn a challenging skill. Try something you admire but have the belief that you couldn't possibly do. Take a chance.

3. Most stressful trait: Procrastinator.

4. The benefit: I am capable of producing amazing things in very short periods of time.

5. Traits to reclaim: Creative, Funny, Spontaneous, Loyal

people-pleasing mindset

The subsequent behavior that is another stress creator and energy sucker is people-pleasing. When you engage in people-pleasing, you are centered on trying to gain outside approval to the point of driving yourself crazy and into a state of utter exhaustion. You may even build up resentment and blame all because you could not say no or did not want to let anyone down or desperately wanted their approval, love or loyalty.

Essentially you are proclaiming to yourself and the world that everyone else is more important than you are–you believe on some level that their needs come first, and yours are last. You think you are needed, but in reality you are using them to make you feel needed and important. Do you find yourself making statements such as, "I have to do this or so and so will be mad at me, or they won't like me!" or "Won't they think I am so awesome if I do this."?

It may be less than obvious to you, but sure signs of this are: over committing, making decisions that are in others or your ex's best interest, or trying to please others at your expense. It is riddled with "I should", "I have to" or "I ought to." You may even feel responsible for making sure their needs get met. Again, this behavior may be totally out of your awareness. However, it interferes with your ability to engage without feeling "uptight" and "stressed."

At the root of it, if this is your mindset, lack self-confidence, and this causes a behavioral pattern that can lead you to a serious illness. Basically as you are putting everyone else's needs in front of your own, your subconscious resentment, anger, and frustration are feeding your stress. Your actions can't make others happy, if it appears to do so, it's only temporarily. Ultimately you are not even in their equation because their happiness is their issue. Therefore, your job is to create your happiness. Isn't it time you take responsibility, meet your needs and start working on producing your joy? You deserve to be happy too, and it is a choice. What is your choice going to be?

Transforming People-Pleasing Mindset Exercise:

(I recommend this even if you think you don't have a people pleaser mindset, we all have behaviors of putting others needs first that hold us back from time to time.)

1. Recognize you have a choice. For the next 21 to 30 days, say NO to all the extra tasks that people approach you with that aren't required by your employer or are not necessary to take care of

yourself, your children, and your responsibilities. Set your priorities. If it is something that you really would enjoy doing, and it can wait a few weeks, do your best to postpone it or pass the opportunity if it doesn't greatly impact your goals and vision. If it is helping an old woman cross the street, by all means, feel free to choose to help her. I'm referring to the huge energy suckers and other stress producers. You are in control of your schedule. You are an adult and can speak up for yourself. It is okay to say NO— the sun will still rise and set, I assure you.

2. Notice how it feels and where it feels in your physical body when you say no. Notice and observe the thoughts that follow saying no.

3. Practice NOT saying you're sorry. People pleasers are chronic at apologizing - for everything. Start with saying sorry less, paying attention and being mindful of how often you say it. Do an experiment and place a semi-loose rubber band around your wrist. Snap it every time you say YES when you mean NO. Snap it every time you say SORRY when you have no reason to apologize. The point is not making painful snaps, snapping the band is just a way of gauging and bringing mindful presence to what is truly going on.

4. At the end of each week, write in a journal about how often you are taking on projects or doing things for others because you feel obligated, want them to like you, or need outside validation. Journal about where in your body you feel uneasy when you say no or where you feel good when you say no. Note how often you have

found yourself snapping that rubber band. By week three, check in to see if there is an improvement. Acknowledge yourself for your progress and if you've made none, start the process over.

What other ways can you support yourself if shifting this mindset and boosting your confidence? I recommend reading these two books, *The Book of No: 250 Ways to Say It—And Mean It and Stop People-Pleasing Forever* by Susan Newman, Ph.D. and the best book I've read on self-confidence, *Courage: Overcoming Fear and Igniting Self-Confidence* by Debbie Ford.

You Can and You Will Thrive if
That is Your Deepest Desire!

Mindsets are crucial in determining what you can and cannot experience in life. We just identified three of the top joy-killers and now it is up to you to step into action seven. We know you are capable of having a happier life and that you are more than capable of creating that for yourself. Now is the time to complete the exercises provided in this chapter in your Thrive Anyway Clarity Journal. For the next 21 days you can also begin the practice of saying "NO" to things you really don't want to spend your energy doing and create a new healthier habit.

If you haven't already downloaded your Thrive Anyway Clarity Journal Go Now To:
www.thriveanywaybook.com

Creating Your Happier Healthier You!

I was so
wrapped up
in his story,
I was blind
to my own.

-Julie Bishop
*"Thrive Anyway: You Can Heal
Your Broken Heart"*

CHAPTER 8

Foursome: Fear, Guilt, Shame, and Regret

The conversation about thriving after a relationship would be incomplete without the discussion of fear, guilt, regret and shame. And most importantly, the stories and beliefs you have created around them. These stories can transform into powerful teachers of healing. Each bearing its own gift, the stories beneath fear, guilt, shame and regret (the foursome) can reveal a part or parts of yourself which are ready for deeper understanding, freedom, and growth. When you are willing to recognize your story is not the totality of who you are, and stop suppressing, hiding and running from the beliefs you've created out of your fear, guilt, shame, and regret you can find freedom. If these stories and views remain unchanged, they retreat into your unconscious awareness, alter your operating system, and begin to validate themselves in the outside world – becoming the root of your self-sabotage.

According to the creator of The Shadow Process and The Shadow Experience and New York Times Best-selling author Debbie Ford - these unconscious beliefs and stories are often formed in childhood. She explains that they were originated to protect you as a result of events you weren't yet equipped to handle or understand. As you grow, you forget you created these beliefs. They become the unconscious drivers that dictate what you can and can't have later in life. They determine what you draw into your life and what you unknowingly repel. These limiting beliefs are magnetic, attracting people and situations into your life to repeatedly verify that they are true. But they are not who, and what you or anyone else is in entirety, they are just beliefs that can change. We often recall the story we create about the events that happen. We keep the story alive and wear it as a badge, using it to explain and justify why new events occur. Such as "I don't fit in anywhere." or "I always attract self-absorbed men." Again, these are just stories that can change if you don't want them to keep showing up, attracting more of the same. You can choose to let them go and create more empowering interpretations and beliefs.

There are distinct differences between fear, guilt, shame and regret, yet they often work together to make up and define the stories we create:

Fear is an emotion caused by the belief that something or someone will likely inflict pain or something unpleasant will happen. Fear that your spouse will leave if they find out you've cheated on them is an example.

Guilt is a bad feeling about something you did, feel that you caused or even something that you did not do but feel you should have done. Guilt is a feeling caused by action or inaction. Such as feeling horrible about cheating on your spouse.

Shame is feeling bad about yourself for something you did or did not do. It is the creator of shadows and disempowering beliefs. It might look like beating yourself up and making your affair mean something about yourself such as "I am a disgusting, cruel bitch."

Regret is often the baby of shame and guilt mixed with the desire to alter the event all together long after the event happened. Regret and shame are the beating sticks; self-abusive inner dialogue you use to keep the fear, shame and guilt alive. The abusive dialogue sounds something like, "If only I could go back and not slept with him, I am so stupid, what was I thinking, what if I lose everything?" What is your inner dialogue saying to you?

The foursome work together to weave a story about yourself, others or the world that become defining for future events. It is often because of unconscious or conscious fear, suppressed guilt, shame or regret that you overeat, overwork, overcommit, or are overly responsible for others. It can also cause you to isolate yourself, have a fear of intimacy, and the inability to express a range of emotion. If you partake in these types of activities, one, some or all of the foursome are running the show in your subconscious. They are the creators of dis-empowering beliefs, shadows, and stories. By questioning, understanding, and shifting the beliefs and stories you create about yourself, others or the world because of your fear, guilt, shame and regret, you can find liberation.

You suppress the foursome because they make you feel uncomfortable. You judge yourself and make the events that create them mean something about yourself such as stupid, jealous, foolish, heartless, to name a few. You are afraid and ashamed someone might find this out and reject you. In fact, you have gone to great lengths to create qualities to hide behind the mask you present to the world, whatever it is you think you are because of them. The pain and fear are so great that you suppress these negative qualities, creating instead, ones that you know will bring you love, respect, and safety. While doing so, you develop some incredible qualities. However, you also reject much of who you are and rob yourself of the ability to be whole. Some characteristics commonly expressed to cover buried parts: an over-achiever, highly independent, strong, bold, loving, or giving - come from judging yourself (or having others judge you) as stupid, incapable, weak, shy, cruel or selfish. By hiding and denying your fear, guilt, shame and regret, you create more pain and struggle because the suppressed parts of you will eventually leak out when you least expect them.

This coping mechanism sounds hopeless, yet fear, guilt, shame and regret are all keys to freedom and growth. You achieve liberation when you lean into them and ask yourself why you feel these to begin with - the answers free you from your pain. Much like when you are driving, and you lose control of your vehicle on ice, the knee-jerk reaction is to turn the wheel away from the direction you are moving when in fact, when on the ice, by driving in the direction the ice is sending you, you gain control. So, instead of hiding, denying and running away from parts of yourself you don't want to be with, negative beliefs, or old stories filled with guilt, regret or shame, you are better off steering directly into and through them.

The beauty of what the foursome holds for you is discovering parts of yourself that need to be acknowledged, embraced and reclaimed. So how do you embrace these suppressed parts of yourself to become whole again? In intimate relationships, it's often the very qualities you judge your partner for that reflect back to you the very things you have forgotten and hidden. Once you identify what they are, you can learn what gifts you have experienced because of them and make a conscious choice to make peace. Let me share two personal examples that impacted one another as I discovered them after the end an intimate relationship.

Different events will trigger your beliefs. They will come out in full force and undermine what is good in your life. When my father and a close friend died this past year, it opened old wounds, beliefs, guilt, shame and regret. Through my initial guilt of not being there for my dying aunt when I was fourteen and my mother when I was sixteen, my shame is what I made my lack of being there for my Dad and friend mean about myself.

What kind of person is not there for those they love when they need them the most? I decided at some point back then; I was heartless and selfish. I had my other qualities of being loving and self-less to mask these seemingly repulsive parts. After a while, I forgot about them, but they were just under the surface waiting to pop up and sabotage me. Forgetting about them or not wanting to own them gives these parts power over you. It's in revealing them, finding their gifts and embracing them as a part of yourself that you regain the power. My parts were triggered once again by my recent losses.

Not being able to face being heartless, my regret enabled me to use my loving, compassionate traits not only because those are better qualities to express but to cover my shame. The regret of not doing more, not being there more, mixed with the shame of feeling heartless inevitably left me exhausted, dependent and vulnerable. I wanted someone else to comfort me as these beliefs and shadows worked beneath my conscious awareness. I wanted someone to validate me – to assure me that I was okay, loveable, and needed.

I could not face these qualities. After all, I was used to presenting to the world my more endearing qualities of confidence, independence, and strength. Heartless, needy and dependent made my stomach turn. I refused to own them, therefore, rejected them, buried them and hoped no one would see them. They popped up regardless. They were not qualities that my former partner had any idea how to handle. I shifted our equilibrium, the balance of our dynamic. No doubt it brought up feelings that made him uncomfortable – possibly mirroring things he wasn't ready to face or own either. The reflection of my qualities may have unconsciously fueled his fears and shadows. They could have easily ignited the need to escape and desire for more space. Possibly they increased his drive to over-work while decreasing his desire to be with me. Either you can run in fear of the beliefs and story born from your guilt, shame, and regret or, you can take them as an opportunity to observe, explore and grow.

Being trained in shadow work – the art of embracing all of your traits both the dark as well as the light, I chose to acknowledge and embrace the qualities of heartless, dependent, and vulnerable. Once I admitted they existed, I discovered the gifts of having these qualities. The gift of heartless was a protection that provided space and time to prepare for the inevitable loss of people I loved deeply. My vulnerability allowed others to connect deeply with me. Being dependent and needy gave others the opportunity and blessing of holding me. In making peace with these parts, and taking action to integrate them in a healthy way; I could impart and share my experience with you.

The last few months or so of our time together, I knew something was off, but couldn't quite place it. When I asked my then partner if anything was going on that we should discuss, the reply was always "I am fine," until one day, he wasn't. Most likely he hadn't been "fine" since I intuitively sensed things weren't right. For him, all he could express was that he longed for his own space, wanted to work on his projects, no longer wanted to share his life or be intimate with me. He admitted that he had been frustrated by realizing this because he was experiencing difficulty understanding why he was feeling this way. He struggled in his mind with the conflict. Admittedly, he recognized we spent a good deal of time apart, were both independent, each possesses most of the qualities we thought we wanted in a partner, and we shared many interests. In silence, this man struggled despite the openness and agreement we had about sharing what was on our minds. Despite having "checked in" several times throughout the months leading to our decision to part ways. The day he did share these things, in his eyes there were shame and guilt. His body language was that of a young boy. I could see and feel that he genuinely felt horrible, yet he also completely believed in his story that he must have something wrong with him. The belief that he couldn't get past his issues had him convinced he needed to end the relationship. He shared that somehow he felt he was broken and damaged when it came to "being in relationships." He expressed being unavailable at this time because of his desire to focus on his career, and it was unfair for us both to continue. He felt I deserved better than that. There was not much room for discussion when a person stands firmly in their conviction. Therefore, we ended the relationship.

The following day, I was in a great deal of pain over this loss and at the same time, bewildered by what I can only describe as a sense of relief. Possibly because it confirmed my intuition had been right on, and partly because I no longer had to wonder why he was so distant. I believed what hurt most was that this person I cared deeply for was hostage to his story - he believes he is broke when it comes to intimate relationships, that he shouldn't be in one. He believes what others have repeatedly told him and what he ultimately tells himself - that he is damaged, something is wrong with him; unconnected, distant, unfeeling, uninterested and numb. These beliefs hold him back from experiencing potentially extraordinary relationships and have, in the past, hurt many he cared about most, including himself. It keeps people at a comfortable distance, and their wanting more of him seems to push him even further away. He is missing the opportunity to work through it with a partner whose life work is transforming beliefs, stories, and shadows to find true liberation. He will continue to attract this dynamic until he uses it to heal and be free. These are the choices he is free to make in his life as are you.

How long do you want to wait to have a healthy and loving relationship? What wounds and beliefs do you need to transform? What could have happened to you to create such powerful beliefs that create the perfect dynamics to prove they are a truth? Possibly something in your life, like his, triggers your story and the beliefs that go with it. Your ego, designed to keep you safe and attract or create the circumstances to prove beliefs to be true, works overtime. Like him, if you and I don't address our belief system of relationships now or in the future, it will continue to impact adversely all of your relationships – with yourself, your children, family, friends and business colleagues –and the relationships will not be as fulfilling as they could.

Begin to look and ask yourself powerful questions to explore. What has happened in your life in regards to all of the relationship that didn't work out well? When is the pain of repeating the same pattern painful enough to make a change or shift in perception? How do you show up in your relationships? What did you make your breakup mean about you? What do you make it mean about the opposite sex?

Whose story has your attention? I was so wrapped up in his story; I was blind to my own. This is typical after a breakup. You tend to think more about the other person and don't focus on what is going on for you. Imagine my surprise, while participating in The Ford Institute's Shadow Experience at Omega in Rhinebeck, New York, I discovered that what I believed about my former partner and was true for me as well. I wanted to believe that his story belonged only to him, but it was a reflection of my own. Your partners and children are often your best mirrors, ripe with discoveries that can help you grow.

It was through internal visualizations working on my guilt, shame, and regrets that I discovered I too had beliefs about myself that were impacting my choices and actions in my relationships. My story plays out differently, but elements were there just the same. I had been unknowingly and repeatedly guarding my heart. I didn't let others in too close, and ultimately created intimate relationships that proved men are not safe, and my heart would be hurt. Utilizing a guided inner voyage, I embarked on a quest of self-inquiry to figure out what had happened to me, what beliefs did I create and what gifts they have given me and what needed transforming for me to move forward. What I discovered shouldn't have shocked me, but it did.

I consciously created this defining story over 30 years ago as the result of rape. The event took place with someone I trusted and admired who took advantage of me during an alcohol-induced blackout. Therefore, at thirteen years old, I kept it a secret because I felt responsible, didn't want anyone to know I drank and lastly I was fearful of upsetting other people's lives, valuing their peace more than my own. Out of fear, guilt, shame and regret, I decided to keep myself safe. I created an emotional barrier men couldn't get through. Underneath my fear, guilt, shame and regret, my beliefs were born and eventually I subconsciously retained them as "men are not safe", "love is not safe", "men will hurt me", and "I can't trust anyone."

The fear and shame from this incident in my teens also reinforced an early childhood shadow belief that I was unlovable. Again, throughout my life, my ego sought and attracted events that would prove this view to be true. Therefore, I was unconsciously choosing to partner with emotionally distant men because I didn't have to let them in too close, and they wouldn't realize I was not fully open and available to them. Unfortunately, this also means they either didn't treat me with respect, did not engage long, or kept emotionally distant so that I was lonely within the relationship. Eventually at the end the relationship my ego gets to prove that the belief I created - men aren't truly safe, men will hurt me, and I am unloveable- is true.

The beauty is, it's only true as long as you believe it. Neither you nor I have to be the victim or the perpetrator of our beliefs. Once you are aware of your patterns of belief, you can shift them. They served to keep you safe when you created it, but it no longer serves you now. You're operating on beliefs created when you were a child or a teenager, and it is time to let them go so you can evolve into the next version of yourself.

Some close friends who I shared this mind-blowing revelation with and knew both of us well laughed and said, "Julie, you seem so warm, loving and emotionally available. You do not seem untrusting, distant, closed off and guarded." And to a degree, they aren't wrong; I am loving and emotional as well. I feel very deeply. Being loving, giving, and emotional are the qualities or parts of me I allow the world to see. Hidden by fear, shame, guilt and regret are the other parts. Just like this former partner, I was emotionally distant and guarded. However, I did this to a different degree than him; it didn't express the same. -Just because someone's behavior is often a mirror of your own, it doesn't mean you express the qualities and beliefs to the same degree or in the same manner. Every relationship you have exists, in part, to teach you more about yourself so you can grow to the next level of being and likewise you're there to be a mirror for the other person. That doesn't mean you will learn the lesson at the same time, your partner or former partner may never grow from it. But you are not responsible for their growth, it is up to you to observe, acknowledge, learn and shift your beliefs.

To help you shift your beliefs, do some inward inquiry with powerful questions. Journal about your answers. I also highly recommend reading books, Why Good People Do Bad Things and The Secret of the Shadow by Debbie Ford. You can work directly with an Integrative Coach, such as myself, whom will assist you in discovering the unconscious shadow beliefs running your life and attend a Shadow Process, the three-day miracle workshop run by the Ford Institute.

Additional Powerful questions to ask yourself:

1.What are your beliefs about your former partner?

2.How do those qualities and beliefs you see in that person show up in your life?

3.Begin exploring your fear, guilt, shame and regrets. Who, what, when, where, why?

4.What took place that caused your fear guilt, shame or regret?

5.What meanings did you create about yourself, others, or situations?

6.What is your shame and regret hiding?

7.What is your biggest fear in relationships?

8.How is your fear, guilt, shame and regret impacting your life and relationships?

9.What belief or quality would be empowering?

10.Set up a coaching call with me or anther coach you feel connect to work through your story and discover what might be sabotaging your life and relationships.

You Can and You Will Thrive if
That is Your Deepest Desire!

There are some very powerful questions in this chapter that you don't want to overlook if you are committed to your own healing. Take some time to go through them and record your answers in the Thrive Anyway Clarity Journal. Then complete the Fearsome Foursome Quiz that is provided in the journal to help you identify the shadow that needs to be reclaimed and brought to the light so that you can move powerful forward in your healing. If you would like assistance in getting to the root of your shadow belief, please consider setting up a one time, free twenty minute call with me at julieannabishop.com. Sometimes, the best way out of your pain is to go in.

If you haven't already downloaded your Thrive Anyway Clarity Journal Go Now To:
www.thriveanywaybook.com

Creating Your Happier Healthier You!

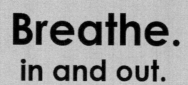

CHAPTER 9

Breathing and Visualizations

A rhythmic breathing and visualization process, when practiced on a consistent basis, is very effective for calming deep-seated grief, mental anxieties, and dis-empowering thoughts. The purpose is to enable you to clear quickly your mental chatter that contributes to stress, tension, worry, and anxiety. It is useful when your mind is racing with negative, fearful, anxious thoughts to transform your thought into the polar opposite with positive, joyful and more uplifting perspectives. Practice this meditative process at least five to ten minutes to receive the maximum benefit.

Believe me, you can't really do visualizations wrong. It may feel awkward at first and difficult to see mental imagery. There have been many clients who shared that it took them a while to visualize anything. Not seeing it clearly is not unusual, some people are more auditory or sensory, and visualizations often take practice and patience. As long as your intention and attention are on this exercise, you will receive benefits. In time, as you relax and become comfortable with the process, you will be able to experience more and more vivid imagery, hear more clearly or sense more deeply depending on the way you process information easiest.

It is best to practice this exercise in a quiet place, free from distractions, where you won't be disturbed. The more times you practice this meditation, the easier it will be to accomplish the same results in busier environments.

Eventually, you will begin to notice a calming effect on your state of mind along with a sensation of peace and relaxation. Sometimes you may be so anxious, which makes visualizing very challenging, but don't give up. That is quite natural and with time, self-patience and practice even you will be able to do this exercise. Be gentle with yourself.

It is recommended to either sit or stand during this visualization. Close your eyes and move all your attention to your breath. To become more aware of your breathing, place one hand on your upper chest and one over your belly button. Take a slow breath and let your stomach swell forward as you inhale and fall back gently as you exhale. Take a similar breath each time to get a steady rhythm going. Your hand on your chest should have little to no movement. Again, attempt to take the same depth of breath on your inhale and exhale. It is often helpful also to develop a cycle where you can count to six when you take a breathe in, pause, and count to eight when you breathe out. These methods will help you focus on your breathing, bring you fully present to the moment and leave no room for other thoughts to come into your mind.

If you are aware of other thoughts entering your mind, notice them, and then let them go as you bring your attention and focus back to your counting and breathing. Continue to do this for a few minutes. Practicing this type of breath pattern strengthens the diaphragmatic muscle and will eventually start to work without thought or effort—leaving you with a nice relaxed feeling all the time.

Now, move your awareness to your feet. Try to feel your feet with your mind. See if you can feel each toe. Close your eyes and picture the base of your feet with roots growing slowly out of the bottom and into the earth beneath you. The roots are growing at a quickening pace and are reaching deep into the soil of the earth. You are now firmly rooted to the ground beneath you. You are a stable large oak tree.

Allow yourself to stay with the feel that you are grounded safely and securely. Once you have created a strong sense of rootedness, like a tree, picture a cloud of bright light forming high above you. Envision this light descending upon you, imagine it ignites a bright white light that spreads down through your head all the way through your body, through your legs and out through the bottom of your feet into the roots of the earth beneath you.

As this white light passes through you, feel it cleansing and clearing all of you–your mind, your body, and your spirit. Imagine that this light is illuminating and dissolving mental noise–toxic, negative and stressful thoughts that you may have been thinking–the dis-empowering chatter and feelings melt and burn away. Repeat this visualization four to five times until you truly sense that you're being cleared and released from your negative anxious thoughts.

Once you have completed the clearing, imagine yourself under a large, gently flowing waterfall. The water is radiant and softly bubbling with life force. As you stand beneath it, you feel the water washing over you, soothing you and completing your cleanse. Open your mouth and let its water refresh your thirst. Hear the sound of the flowing water as it hits the rocks around you. This water is life itself, washing away stress. With heartfelt gratitude thank yourself, the roots, the light, the water for your cleanse. Allow yourself to hear a word or short empowering message that you can post in your home, your vehicle or work that you can look to when your thoughts turn into self-defeating chatter. When you have your word or short mantra, you are ready to step out of the water and slowly open your eyes, coming back to the room fully awake and alert.

Your mind is like a muscle, to relax, it needs to be stimulated to release what it is holding. The more realistic the imagined visualization, the more benefit you will gain. Many clients report very beneficial and soothing results from using simple meditations such as this, and it is always the favorite part of my classes, workshops, and coaching. The great thing about these guided meditations is that you can change the elements to fit your preferences. You can imagine a river instead of a waterfall, or floating on a lake. Use any situation or location that you find calming, a garden, a beach, a meadow or a forest, just find your "happy place," and go there. Just make sure wherever you picture in your mind—it is a place that feels safe, calm and relaxing.

By visualizing different situations, you are allowing your mind to release. It is like sending a message to your brain that when you close your eyes and begin - it is a time to let go of anything you are holding onto mentally, including the anxious thinking. It is important to incorporate a regular practice of this, one time per day, to train your mind in how to let go of the stress. With practice, you can learn to relax within minutes of starting this type of meditation. Your daily practice can take place just before bed if you have trouble sleeping or first thing in the morning if you start your day out frazzled. Maybe it is midday during the chaos of work and demands that you need to find a place to do your breathing and visualization exercise. Engage in this technique when you need it the most.

This tool is not the best technique to end an anxiety attack, but it can prevent attacks from beginning. It supports the riddance of uncomfortable sensations. If carried out, it promotes a deep feeling of inner peace and is very effective in dealing with overall mental stress. You can download a recording of this exercise to listen to as you are just beginning—it can be very helpful just to follow a voice instead of trying to do it all on your own.
ww.thriveanywaybook.com/bonuses

You Can and You Will Thrive if
That is Your Deepest Desire!

Are you ready to deeply relax and let go of your worry, stress, and fears for a more favorable experience? Great, we thought you'd never ask. The ninth step you can take to support yourself is to download our recording that leads you through the visualization provided in this chapter. It can be downloaded with the other supportive bonuses at:

www. thriveanywaybook.com/bonuses.

If you haven't already downloaded your Thrive Anyway Clarity Journal Go Now To:
www.thriveanywaybook.com

Begin Creating Your Happier Healthier You!

Use your broken heart as a kick-ass catalyst to grow.

-Julie Bishop
"Thrive Anyway: You Can Heal Your Broken Heart"

CHAPTER 10

Healing and Support

In our society, we seek the quick fix. However, there is nothing speedy about healing a broken heart. It takes time and energy to move through all the stages of grief that come with the end of an intimate relationship. The beauty is that you have a choice, you don't have to get stuck and spin your wheels; you have an opportunity to open yourself up to new possibilities for your life. Believe it or not, you are actually at a crossroads. You have two paths you can travel down during the grieving process, similar to the choices you have in managing your stress. Everyone needs time to be sad about their loss. Room to weep and grieve is a healthy part of the process. There will come a moment when you need to decide how you are going to view your break up. Are you going to use it as a kick-ass catalyst to grow, expand and learn or a beating stick to make all kinds of negative and disempowering beliefs about yourself? The choice belongs to no one but you. Choose wisely, and you will be creating a fulfilling new life for yourself. Making the breakup mean 'I am unlovable', 'broken', 'no good at relationships', or that 'there really must be something wrong with me' will only make for a long, painful, struggle and will only attract another mate into your life that will prove those things true. When a person breaks up with you, ultimately, deep down, it mostly has nothing to do with you exactly. It is about what is going on inside of them; they are suffering from their needs or fears. If you were the one breaking-up with someone else, you might honestly believe it was about them or something they've done but deep down, it was mostly about you, your needs or fears.

Take an inventory of your needs, desires, and dreams. Old habits, patterns, beliefs and fears will keep you repeating the same old scenarios over and over so list them out as well. List out your fears and your beliefs about your former partner. How many of your fears are real and how many of those things you blame or believe about your partner are true about you to one degree or another? Now is your chance to make brave new choices for how you will move forward in your life and your future relationships. The other great news is that you can move the process along by actively engaging, learning and getting support from those who understand and are also going through a major breakup or divorce.

The final and most powerful thing you can learn to do is learn to connect, communicate and listen to the inner wisdom within you. The easiest way out of your pain and the dark place you are in is to go inside. The fastest way out is in. Inside of you are the answers to your needs and your fears. Look inside yourself, into your heart in order to find your path to freedom. Not in your thoughts or mind, but a deeper place within you, your subconscious. How? It can be accomplished through meditation, guided visualization, journaling, hypnotism or journeying to name a few.

You can discover the meaning making, find the negative beliefs about yourself, and uncover your deepest fears. You can take the time to review what your past relationship(s) have taught you about what you don't want and how you don't desire to be treated moving forward. Equally important is to identify what did work for you and how you do want others to treat you. From this sacred and wise place within you, ask yourself some serious questions about what actions, patterns or habits can you shift to ensure that you are treating yourself with the value, love, and respect that you desire to receive. Imagine your ideal, visualize it, journal about it, discuss it with a friend. Then, determine what actions you can take now and over the next several weeks to start moving towards a new vision for yourself and your relationships.

Having a partner to share life with can be wonderful. However, all we need and all we desire we must first learn to find and source from within ourselves. It is no one else's job to "complete" you - that paradigm may be popular but isn't sustainable. It isn't someone else's responsibility to be your "end all be all" or just as importantly it's not your job to be theirs. Improving your relationship with yourself is the path that will lead you to freedom, healing, and the love of your life. There are many books, workshops, and professionals that can assist you with creating a healthy dynamic. I discuss loving and creating a confident relationship with yourself in my upcoming book, Sacred Self-Care: The Stress-Free Art of Loving Yourself; How Applying Self-Compassion, Practicing Self-Acknowledgment, and Improving Self Esteem Can Change the World. Being emotionally healthy inside and out is your key to real freedom, peace of mind and happiness.

Relationships can't begin, exist or fall apart without both parties contributing on some level, consciously or subconsciously. Therefore, another key element to your healing process is to identify how you helped create the dynamic in your past relationship that ultimately didn't work. That knowledge holds the keys to what you have to work on before getting involved with any future partner. If you don't heal the wounds or get the lesson that this relationship had to offer, you will very likely continue to repeat the same pattern. Is it worth repeating or are you ready to get different results your next time around?

For example, in my client Jill's relationship, she was a people-pleasing enabler. She continually put her partner Ted's needs before her own (he never asked her to do this - though she admits he seemed to enjoy it.) She just perceived his needs and took care of them. Her actions enabled him to do less and less for himself. Jill understood Ted's inaction as his lack of partnership, love and caring. The less he did, the more Jill did. In a way, unintentionally, Jill robbed Ted of the opportunity to grow and learn to be more self-reliant and to give. She robbed herself of his ability to express love through action despite her belief that she was helping him. She didn't recognize or even see that her needs were of equal value. Jill also didn't realize that she first needed to meet her needs and quite honestly,

Ted needed to do the same for himself. Ted happened to display a lack of responsibility for himself, which complicated matters. At the age of thirty-seven, he was certainly old enough to take care of himself, his emotions and personal affairs. Fortunately for both of them, when they identified the lack of emotional immaturity and the over-enabling, they were able to accept personal responsibility and work towards modifying their behaviors so they could heal what was pulling them apart. It doesn't always turn out that way.

Sometimes, like Jill and Ted, you can figure this out together and make the necessary shifts together. More often, as one chooses to do their inner work and grow, the other chooses on some level, for many varying reasons including fear of the unknown, to not put in the necessary effort, therefore, not to grow. When this happens, they ultimately bring imbalance to their relationship that often brings it to an end. It doesn't mean you need to keep repeating whatever dynamic it is that ended your relationship. You can heal and move on. I highly recommend Debbie Ford's book, Spiritual Divorce, for its valuable exercises and techniques to help you discover your contribution to the breakdown in your relationship. However, if you had an abusive partner, there is a whole set of powerful emotions, beliefs, and responsibility that you must take into account.

How do you know if you were in an emotionally abusive relationship? Let's go back to the above relationship. If Jill's partner had been knowingly manipulating her to do more out of entitlement or twisted all their arguments back to her being at fault or consistently skirted responsibility favoring blame then most likely there is a level of emotional abuse. He may believe he has the right to control Jill or doesn't see her needs as important as his own (self-centered and selfish) If that resonates, I suggest reading Lundy Bancroft's book, Why Does He Do That? Inside The Minds Of Angry And Controlling Men, and Patricia Evan's books, The Verbally Abusive Relationship, and Victory Over Verbal Abuse. Lundy Bancroft provides a profile of ten types of abusers - many of whom fly under the radar because most of us believe only in the popular stereotype of a batterer depicted in Hollywood. These books help you identify if you were in an abusive dynamic as well as provides red flags and ways to pick up on potential abusers early in future relationships when their behavior is much more subtle. Imperative knowledge as you move forward with your life.

You are worthy of a healthy, loving relationship with yourself and with another when the timing is right. Now is the ideal time to reclaim your life and the gifts you contributed to in your past relationship(s). Acknowledge yourself for all the things you did right. Make a list of all the various ways you loved, were thoughtful, giving, humorous and adventurous. Celebrate what you have to offer, your attributes and qualities that are worth acknowledging. Strengthen your perspective of yourself with these insights. If you are struggling, talk with a close friend who will be honest with you about yourself and your best attributes. In chapter eleven, I discuss ten ideal qualities in a healthy partner that is a good place to begin.

Next, give space for the nine stages of grief. It may take six months, a year or more, but allow yourself to move through your natural grieving process. Surround yourself with those that will support you and give you positive feedback. Begin also to create your own space. Remove whatever reminds you of your former partner in your living space. Is there music you need to part with, pictures that can go, routines or rituals that can be let go of, or shows that you no longer need to watch? Whatever it is, have fun with removing the traces and things that invoke memories of the past to make room for the present and the future.

So where do you go from here you ask? My question to you is where are you in your process? Close your eyes, take a deep breath and be completely honest with yourself. Ask yourself some of the following questions, answer the statements and tune it to what resonates with you right now:

1. What would best support me where I am right now? (Have fun, self-care, connect to others, create, cry, celebrate, learn something new, focus on the kids, etc...)

2. Am I ready to complete any of the exercises in this guide? Which ones?

3. Which of the recommended material am I drawn to read?

4. Join a support group.

5. Participate in a workshop.

6. Talk with a close friend.

7. Talk to a relationship therapist.

8. Work with a coach specializing in relationships or self-confidence.

9. Find a creative outlet to express my feelings.

10. Receive deep bodywork that will help me process my grief and release emotion trapped in my body.

11. Schedule suggested activities on my calendar for the next three months.

12. Support during your healing process is vital. Discover and ask each day—what can I do today to nurture and take care of me?

When you are taking care of you, you will have the energy and desire to care of those in your life that need it. Think of yourself as a pitcher of lemonade. If you keep filling the "glasses" for your children, family, friends, or colleagues without replenishing your "pitcher", how much lemonade are you going to be able to share? What quality will it be? I recommend that you learn to keep your pitcher full, if not, overflowing.

Your support system is vital to your success and speed in healing your heart as well as your ability to give and love others. What is it going to take for you to thrive? If you haven't already, please download your gift, 50 ways to bring more joy, relaxation and self-love (self-value) to kick-start your healing process.

You Can and You Will Thrive if
That is Your Deepest Desire!

Great Work!! By this point in Thrive Anyway, if you have been taking one action step at a time, you are seeing a light at the end of your tunnel. If you feel like you aren't even close, please don't despair, your process just may take a little longer. Resist the urge to compare yourself to others and continue to be kind, patient, and gentle with yourself. There were many great next steps provided within this chapter, so your call to action is to pick one of them and work on it over the next week. Be sure to record your answers and progress in your Thrive Anyway Clarity Journal. Take it one step further and share it online at the community page www.facebook.com/thriveanyway or create a buddy by reaching out to another one of the participants on that page.

If you haven't already downloaded your Thrive Anyway Clarity Journal Go Now To:
www.thriveanywaybook.com

Begin Creating Your Happier Healthier You!

A healthy
relationship
never requires
sacrificing your friends,
loved ones, dreams,
or your dignity.

CHAPTER 11

10 Traits of a Healthy Partner

I n many ways, all of your past relationships provided you with the knowledge of what works and what doesn't. You know how you want someone to show up and exactly the manner in which you don't want them to show up. The same applies to you - you have discovered the areas where you struggle and want to improve. So how do you know you are ready for a new partner? What makes a healthy partner? What exactly do you need to work on in yourself to be a healthier partner? I'm going to share what I've learned and pieced together for myself and give you permission to use it as a baseline as you create one for yourself.

One of the most frequent questions clients ask is, "How do I know I'm ready to date?" There are a few ways to get to the truth of the matter. There are two that I particularly find as good guides. You are ready for a new partner when physically, mentally, and emotionally dating does not feel like you are cheating on your former partner. If you feel like you are cheating, your heart, mind or body hasn't fully let go or come to terms with the loss of the former relationship. You have more work to do. Another way to know you are ready for a new partner is to be absolutely comfortable being single and alone. You don't "need" another person in your life, but having one would be nice. If you feel lonely and desperate for a partner, turn it inward and see how you can be a partner to yourself. If you believe you pass these two inquiries and are ready to date, then you want to identify what you would like to attract and manifest in a relationship and partner.

Each one of us has five to ten core values that are so important to us that they actually subconsciously impact whether or not we get along with others. While you might easily identify with many more, you can usually boil it down to a core group. The more alignment others values are with your own, the better you will get along. Most of us desire to be in healthy relationships. Holding too high of standards might eliminate someone who has the potential for becoming a healthy partner. In the attempt to not exclude these individuals, you will need to determine which traits you are willing to be flexible and what healthy boundaries you need to establish to make it work. Remember we are not perfect and should not hold others to standards we aren't living to either. Be cautious to not use your list to keep you from moving forward with another person out of your fear of actually having a healthy relationship. That said, here is my top ten list:

1. **Supportive and Communicative**. Healthy partners are able to listen to you, hear you and find ways to support your emotions, dreams and being. Healthy partners are your natural cheerleaders or fans who can get behind you and encourage you. They are not into mocking, judging or belittling what is important to you. When you are both supportive and communicate with respect, patience, and understanding in a positive clear way, it builds trust and connection.

2. **Empathetic**. Healthy partners can put themselves in your shoes and attempt to understand what you may be going through with compassion and support. They give you space, hold you, or listen to your needs. Keep in mind you may need to communicate exactly what you need - very few people are mind readers. When you both are empathetic, communicating with respect for each other's wants, views, and emotions allow you both to feel understood and validated.

3. **Authentic and Honest with Integrity**. Healthy partners don't display big discrepancies between their actions and their words. Healthy partners need to really know themselves -

their challenges, their gifts, their limits and intentions. They are able to be upfront and honest with themselves as well as their partners. Authenticity is about honest representation and being you. Honesty and integrity are worth striving for continually within your relationship. When you both can be in integrity, authentic and honest with each other, it builds depth, trust, ease, great communication and connection in the relationship.

4. **Friendly.** A healthy partner is friendly with your family, loved ones, and friends. They actually desire to get to know the important people in your life and make attempts to connect with them or understand them. They protect and nourish their relationship with you. If you find yourself in a disagreement, they don't fly off the handle, become totally despaired, demean you or threaten you in any way. The friendly person is generally nice to others, including strangers. An easy indicator of the level of friendly can be seen in observing how they treat your waiters or waitresses as well as other service professionals. When you are both friendly you will experience the world, each other and everyone else with a positive attitude and creates opportunities for happiness and joy.

5. **Respectful.** A healthy partner treats you with sensitivity and respect. They honor your boundaries and listen to your needs when it comes to the boundaries. They do not try to manipulate or control your behavior. Your perspectives are valued and they are

considerate of your feelings. Ideal partners do not try to change you and allow you to be your own person. Being respectful of each other enables you both to be true to yourselves, to communicate effectively and build trust.

6. **Open and Accepting**. Healthy partners are approachable, undefended and willing to be vulnerable. No one is perfect, but finding a partner that is receptive to feedback and gracious at giving it is a big asset. Being open and accepting enables them to be expressive of thoughts, feelings, and desires as well as open to growth. Relationships evolve and having a partner that is open enables him or her to roll with the changes and make adjustments with you. When both of you are open, you can truly get to know each other and build a very deep, powerful bond.

7. **Independent.** Healthy partners are able to stand on their own, being whom they are and not what others expect or want them to be. They maintain their unique and individual identity both within their relationships as well as with their friends. They have their own individual friends and experiences outside of their intimate relationships. When both partners are able to be independent, it increases or maintains their individual sense of self-worth and respect for one another. They are free to do things on their own or others without resentments, tears, and conflict so each can communicate this freely. Healthy partners can come and go without suspicion or concern from the other about where they

are going, who they are with or what time they will be home because they are open and honest about it. This builds trust and allows both individuals the ability to maintain their individual identities, pursue their own dreams and know they have their partners' love and support.

8. **Mature.** In order for a healthy partnership to occur or for the embodiment of the before mentioned traits, healthy partners must have a certain level of maturity. They make active and transparent efforts to recognize and resolve issues from their past, issues that arise in the present and issues that come up between you. They are emotionally mature and are not looking for you to complete them in any way as they are taking on that responsibility for themselves. This enables healthy partners to be independent, maintain their autonomy as they share life as equals. Naturally if you both are emotionally mature you are able to create a solid and rewarding relationship together.

9. **Affectionate and Passionate**. Everyone has different levels of affection and passion that they are comfortable with, so this does not mean that healthy partners need to be overflowing with these traits. It does indicate that healthy partners find it easy and effortless to be affectionate, responsive and passionate on multiple levels and in relation to their partners' needs. Physically, emotionally and verbally, healthy partners can uninhibitedly receive, respond and outwardly demonstrate affection and warmth.

When both healthy partners are able to give and receive this pleasure, affection, and closeness then they are able to share a deeply satisfying bond.

10. **Positivity and Humor**. These two traits go hand in hand with their ability to fill in when other traits fall short. Healthy partners are often more naturally optimistic and are able to find the good in everything and everyone which makes problem-solving, challenges and hurdles easier to maneuver. Using humor with positivity is a successful combination that enables laughter in the best of times and during the difficult. One cannot underestimate the importance of being able to laugh at oneself. When both partners have healthy senses of humor and are able to come from a positive perspective, they cultivate joy, happiness, and fun in their relationship.

As I mentioned previously, no relationship is perfect and we can't expect each other to be perfect either. We are always growing and evolving and so are our relationships. These are based on the traits and values I find important in my life. Some of these may not be what are most important to you. Spend some time brainstorming traits and creating your list. You can begin by going through it and circling twenty of the traits that matter to you. Begin with the ones that you want to be known for and would love to have a friend say about you. Keep narrowing it down to the top ten most important traits and that is your list of values you will find refreshing in a partner. Rate yourself on a level of one to ten, one being not so great at expressing the trait and ten being you live the expression of the trait. Those scoring under a seven are the areas you can begin to work on within yourself.

You Can and You Will Thrive if
That is Your Deepest Desire!

Healthy you attracts a healthy partner! This chapter was my top ten list and now your eleventh action step is to write your list of characteristics in your Thrive Anyway Clarity Journal. There is a long list of attributes already provide for you in the journal. Circle the ones that are most important to you. Then narrow your list to the Top 10. You don't have to put them in order of preference, but you can rate yourself on a scale of 1 to 10. One being "Not at all" and ten being have this trait 100%. If you fall below a seven, journal about ways that you could increase that quality in your own life.

If you haven't already downloaded your Thrive Anyway Clarity Journal Go Now To:
www.thriveanywaybook.com

Creating Your Happier Healthier You!

My Mission in life
is not merely to survive,
but to thrive: and to do
so with some passion,
some compassion,
and some style.

- Maya Angelou,
American Author

CHAPTER 12

Conclusion: Where Do I Go From Here?

There are numerous ways to nurture your broken heart and support yourself through your healing process. This book has provided tools, ideas, and shifts to ensure you have the ability to do just that. Throughout this book you have learned to:

- Handle your stress so it isn't handling you.

- Recognize, understand and deal with each phase of your grief.

- Set healthy boundaries so your next relationship is the best.

- Tame negative, fault-finding, and people-pleasing mindsets.

- Visualize and self-hypnotize gain clarity and peace of mind.

- Identify characteristics and values of healthy partners so you can become one as well as know how to identify one in the future.

- Develop your core values so you can experience the greatest love of your life – your own and others.

With this knowledge comes responsibility. Only you can implement what you've learned and create a life you love and create healthy partnerships. Please resist the urge to curl up in a ball and stay in bed for six weeks or months. If ever there were a time that you could make a big change in your life, it is now. You have a clean slate, a whole new canvas, and a new chapter in your life waiting for you to create whatever you want and desire for yourself. What are you going to do with it? If that thought scares you, find someone to help you embrace it rather than repel from it. If it excites you, go for it and play full out!

Maybe you are still carrying residual bitterness, anger and pain about how things ended, but at some point, know that holding on to that for too long without release will erode, discolor, infect, and bring toxins into your future experiences. It is imperative that you let it all go as you begin to heal and move forward with your life. You deserve to thrive in every way, shape and form. Know that you are not alone, that millions share this journey with you. In fact, I'm out here holding a sacred space for your process; cheering, praying, chanting, meditating, dancing, yelling, drumming, walking on fire, toasting and celebrating you and your newest adventure.

If you need further help and support and want me to partner directly with you feel free to sign up for a personal and direct 20-minute discovery session designed to propel you forward with immediate actions at www.thriveanywaybook.com/coachme. We also offer group coaching, intimate six-month coaching in exclusive small VIP groups or take my online courses "Breakup Boot Camp" or attend one of my one day or weekend workshops. Be sure to sign up for your bonus gifts and you will receive periodic emails from me regarding these and the latest offerings.

Plan out your next moves once you've done the steps in this book. Your goal is to: THRIVE ANYWAY– let no one hold you back– not even yourself!

You Can and You Will Thrive if
That is Your Deepest Desire!

Woo Hoo!!! You made it through Thrive Anyway and
have gathered all kinds of tools and clarity to assist you in
your healing process. Congratulations, you now have a
choice in the direction your extraordinary life goes in. If
you are really brave email your journal and be apart of our
inner circle for the next book in the Thrive Anyway book
series. All journal submitted for the giveaway will remain
completely anonymous.

Thrive Anyway - Clarity Journal Bi-Annual Give-away
One journal entry will be chosen at random every 6
months to receive 9 private coaching sessions at no cost.
Enter your journal today: to julie@julieannabishop.com.

If you haven't already downloaded your Thrive
Anyway Clarity Journal Go Now To:
www.thriveanywaybook.com

Begin Creating Your Happier Healthier You!

Bibliography

[1]American Psychological Association's Stress in America™ Survey, retrieved from http://www.apa.org/news/press/releases/stress/2014/stress-report.pdf and http://www.apa.org/news/press/releases/2015/02/money-stress.aspx February 4, 2015

[2]American Psychological Association's Stress in America™ Survey, retrieved from http://www.apa.org/news/press/releases/stress/2014/stress-report.pdf

[3] American Psychological Association's Stress in America™ Survey, retrieved from http://www.apa.org/news/press/releases/stress/2014/stress-report.pdf

[4] Benson, Herbert (2010), *Relaxation Revolution*, New York, Scribner, Division of Simon & Schuster Inc.

[5]Center For Disease Control http://www.cdc.gov

[6] ADAA, Anxiety and Depression Association of American, retrieved from http://www.adaa.org/understanding-anxiety

[7] National Inst. of Mental Health, retrieved from http://www.nimh.nih.gov/index.shtml

[8] National census, retrieved from http://www.census.gov

[9] US statistics Center For Disease Control, retrieved from http://www.cdc.gov

[10] American Psychological Association's Stress in America™ Survey, retrieved from http://www.apa.org/news/press/releases/stress/2014/stress-report.pdf

[11] http://www.healthinsightstoday.com

[12] ADDA, "Facts and Statistics," Anxiety and Depression Association of America, retrieved from

[13] Holland, Judy (2015), *Moody Bitches: The Truth About the Drugs You're Taking, the Sleep You're Missing, the Sex You're Not Having, and What's Really Making You Crazy*, New York, Penguin Press

Recommended Resources

Reform Your Inner Mean Girl: 7 Steps to Stop Bullying Yourself and Start Loving Yourself, by Amy Ahlers and Christine Arlyo

Should I Stay or Should I Go?, by Lundy Bancroft

Why Does He Do That?, by Lundy Bancroft

The Relaxation Revolution, by Herbert Benson, MD

The Mind/Body Effect, by Herbert Benson, MD

Timeless Healing: The Power and Biology of Belief, by Herbert Benson, MD

Welcome to Your Crisis: How to Use the Power of Crisis to Create the Life You Want, by Laura Day

The Forgiveness Handbook, A Simple Guide to Freedom of the Mind and Heart, by Clifford B. Edwards

The Verbally Abusive Relationship, by Patricia Evans

Victory over Verbal Abuse, by Patricia Evans

Courage: Overcoming Fear and Igniting Self-Confidence, by Debbie Ford

Spiritual Divorce, by Debbie Ford

The Best Year of Your Life, by Debbie Ford

Why Good People Do Bad Things, by Debbie Ford

The Dark Side of the Light Chasers, by Debbie Ford

Moody Bitches: The Truth about the Drugs You're Taking, the Sleep You're Missing, the Sex You're Not Having, and What's Really Making You Crazy, by Dr. Julie Holland, MD

Happiness is a Choice, by Barry Kaufman

A Thousand Names for Joy, by Byron Katie

On Death and Dying, by Dr. Elisabeth Kübler-Ross

Book of No: 250 Ways to Say It—and Mean It and Stop People-Pleasing Forever, by Susan Newman, Ph.D.

The Think Big Manifesto: Think You Can't Change Your Life (and the World)? Think Again, by Michael Port and Mina Samuels

The Art of Extreme Self-Care, by Cheryl Richardson

Radical Self-forgiveness, by Colin Tipping

Links and downloads

www.thriveanywaybook.com/bonuses

www.wrf.org/alternative-therapies/science-of-breath.php

www.eftfree.net/get-the-eftfree-manual-2/

www.psychologytoday.com/articles/200304/the-benefits-meditation

www.naturalnews.com/036313_meditation_depression_brain_function

www.mixcloud.com/search/?mixcloud_query=meditation

www.mixcloud.com/search/?mixcloud_query=guided+meditation

www.journeydancehq.com

About Julie Anna Bishop

Julie Anna Bishop

Client Proclaimed Kick-Ass Courage Coach ™

I graduated from the State University of New York at Purchase in 1991, with a degree in anthropology and photography. At SUNY Purchase I refused to conform to those who seemed to be conforming to the "non-conformity"; I was a misfit in the land of misfits- hiding my colorfulness on the interior, instead of on my hair or skin. Entering the work world, I found myself dedicated to the human services field for five years before transforming into a recognized leader in the field of universal and sustainable interior design; creating healthy and sacred interiors while assisting manufacturing companies redesign their product lines to fulfill the needs of the end users. To prove my worth, I climbed the corporate ladder arriving at the Vice Presidency role of a commercial design firm before jumping off the corporate track to begin an interior lifestyle design firm (with a very cool partner, Mary Mosner) to serve the private and senior living sectors with a holistic, healthy approach to design. After becoming a mother (my most sacred role), I became a nationally certified massage therapist and Certified Integrative Coach, training for several years with spiritual leader Debbie Ford and her mentors Kelley Kosow, Julie Stroud, Jeff Malone, Cliff Edwards, and Fran Fusco at the Ford Institute.

Slowly, I traded designing interior spaces of buildings and homes for assisting others in redesigning their own interior well-being. I found myself back in the service of human and spiritual beings. In addition, I have also trained with New York Best Selling Author and Business Coach, Michael Port and Best Selling Author and Business Coach, Jenny Fenig. I continue to be a life learner as well as a teacher.

Some of my professional accomplishments include being a contributing author to two Amazon Best Sellers, The Gratitude Book Project: Celebrating 365 Days of Gratitude, and The

Gratitude Book Project: Celebrating Motherhood. I was a highlighted healthy mindset coach by Michael Port's tele-festival, "Book Yourself Solid Amplified." And have been acknowledged for my contribution to Debbie Ford's 9th book, Courage: Igniting Self-Confidence.

It was during my contribution to Debbie's research for Courage that I was able to find the courage within to face what I had been avoiding, the unhealthy dynamic of my then marriage. It has been the journey of leaving, surviving and then thriving that has added richness and depth to my work as a coach. I have learned the gift of receiving and surrendering. And most importantly, I know the depth of my inner strength which enabled me to transform all the chaos, pain, and struggle into an amazing new life filled with supportive friends, family, and new opportunities. I found true love in the most unexpected of places- within myself, my children, and those I am closest too. I can think of nothing I would rather do that continue to show others how to do the same
for themselves.

THANK YOU TO EDWARD ACKER PHOTOGRAPHY FOR
HEAD SHOTS AND FAMILY PHOTO

WWW.EDWARDACKERPHOTOGRAPHER.COM/

Invatation
To the Reader

If you are a someone dedicated to your growth, a creative ripple maker, a powerful agent of change, or a passionate visionary who is experiencing life's stresses and unexpected events, you can rise above the challenge. If you are going through a divorce, lost a loved one or have lost yourself, you can learn how to use your struggle as a springboard. Possibly you are just starting to burn out from superwoman/man over-excursion, whatever you're up against - you can become a courageous rising Phoenix - one who rises from the ashes to:

● Manifest self-care, deep self-worth, and authentic esteem - so you can face life from a position of strength.

● Alchemize your heartache and trauma into energy that works for you and not against you. Sharpen your badass edge, fuel for your juicy tank of creativity, and perform at your highest so you can thrive in every aspect of your life.

- Handle your stress so it isn't handling you. Unleash your highest energy, compassion and integrity from within by learning to listen to your innate wisdom instead of searching for all the answers "out there" or waiting for someone to come "save" you.

- I am committed to supporting you to take charge of your personal crisis, gain unshakable self-confidence, and reconnect to your inner wisdom so you can build a meaningful, fulfilling life according to your terms.

- Join one of our group coaching, individual coaching or VIP coaching programs with a private, exclusive bad-ass retreat or find someone who resonates with you and work with them.

Just do something to support yourself. It's time to embrace your kick-ass self and thrive!

With love,

JulieAnnaBishop.com

Julie Anna Bishop, client proclaimed "Kick-ass" Courage Coach™, Courageous Warrior of Love, Visionary, Alchemist, Author, Speaker and Certified Integrative Leader and Coach™

To find out more visit
www.julieannabishop.com

Join her on Facebook at
https://www.facebook.com/julieannabishop.author

Join our community at https://www.facebook.com/thriveanyway

For questions or inquiries about collaboration, workshops, speaking events, or any other subject please email her directly - julie@julieannabishop.com